First World War
and Army of Occupation
War Diary
France, Belgium and Germany

40 DIVISION
Divisional Troops
231 Field Company Royal Engineers
3 June 1916 - 31 March 1918

WO95/2601/1

The Naval & Military Press Ltd
www.nmarchive.com
Published in association with The National Archives

Published by

The Naval & Military Press Ltd

Unit 10 Ridgewood Industrial Park,

Uckfield, East Sussex,

TN22 5QE England

Tel: +44 (0) 1825 749494

www.naval-military-press.com

www.nmarchive.com

This diary has been reprinted in facsimile from the original. Any imperfections are inevitably reproduced and the quality may fall short of modern type and cartographic standards.

© Crown Copyright
Images reproduced by permission of The National Archives, London, England, 2015.

Contents

Document type	Place/Title	Date From	Date To
Heading	WO95/2601/1		
Heading	40th Division 231st Field Coy R.E. Jun 1916-Mar 1919. To 3 Div Troops		
War Diary	Blackdown	03/06/1916	03/06/1916
War Diary	Naure	04/06/1916	05/06/1916
War Diary	Rigny les Aries	06/06/1916	07/06/1916
War Diary	Drouvin	09/06/1916	09/06/1916
War Diary	Les Brebis	09/06/1916	30/06/1916
Heading	War Diary of 231st Field Company R.E. 40th Div from 1st July 1916 to 31st July 1916		
War Diary	La Gauchiette	01/07/1916	04/07/1916
War Diary	Les Brebis	05/07/1916	31/07/1916
Heading	War Diary of 231st (Field) Coy R.E. from Aug 1st 1916 to Aug 31st 1916 Volume 3		
War Diary	Les Brebis	01/08/1916	30/09/1916
Heading	War Diaries 231st Field Company R.E. October. 1916 Volume V		
War Diary	Philosophe & 14 Bis Village Line	01/10/1916	31/10/1916
Heading	War Diary 231st Field Company RE November, 1916 Volume VI		
War Diary	Houvelin	01/11/1916	01/11/1916
War Diary	Ococh	02/11/1916	03/11/1916
War Diary	Rougefay	04/11/1916	04/11/1916
War Diary	Montegny	05/11/1916	05/11/1916
War Diary	Dormart-En-Ponthieu	06/11/1916	23/11/1916
War Diary	Vauchelle	24/11/1916	25/11/1916
War Diary	Buigny L'Abbe	26/11/1916	30/11/1916
Heading	War Diary of 231st Field Coy R.E. December 1916 Volume VII		
War Diary	Buigny L'Abbe	01/12/1916	09/12/1916
War Diary	Sailly Le-Sec	10/12/1916	28/12/1916
War Diary	Domino-Dump	29/12/1916	31/12/1916
Heading	War Diary of 231st Field Company RE Month of January 1917 Volume VIII		
War Diary	Domino Dump nr Maurepas B 15.62.4	01/01/1917	19/01/1917
War Diary	Domino Dump B 15 b 2.4.	19/01/1917	31/01/1917
Heading	A.P. C2118 War Diary 231st (Field) Company RE. February 1917		
War Diary	Camp 161 A 30b 6.4. Near Curlu	01/02/1917	28/02/1917
Heading	231st Field Company R.E. War Diaries Vol 10		
War Diary	Camp 161 A. 30. B. 6.4 Near Curlu	01/03/1917	20/03/1917
War Diary	Little Dale	21/03/1917	31/03/1917
Heading	War Diary Vol XI 231st (Field) Company R.E. April 1917		
Heading Miscellaneous	40th Division		
War Diary	Little Dale Barracks B. 30. b.	01/04/1917	05/04/1917
War Diary	Etricourt	06/04/1917	30/04/1917
War Diary	Etricourt	08/04/1917	17/04/1917

Heading	231st Field Co. R.E. War Diary from 1st May 1917 To 31st May 1917 Volume 12		
War Diary	Dessart Wood	01/05/1917	13/05/1917
War Diary	Heudicourt	14/05/1917	22/05/1917
War Diary	Dessart Wood	23/05/1917	30/06/1917
Heading	War Diary 231 Field Co RE July 1917 Vol 14		
Miscellaneous			
War Diary	Dessart Wood	01/07/1917	29/07/1917
War Diary	Danum Ravine	30/07/1917	31/07/1917
Heading	War Diary of 231st Field Company R.E. from 1st August 1917 to 31st August 1917		
War Diary	Danum Ravine	01/08/1917	31/08/1917
Heading	War Diary of 231st (Field) Company R.E. September 1917 Volume No 16		
War Diary	Danum Ravine	01/09/1917	31/10/1917
War Diary	Equancourt	01/11/1917	18/11/1917
War Diary	Beaulencourt	19/11/1917	20/11/1917
War Diary	Beaumetz Les Cambrai	21/11/1917	23/11/1917
War Diary	Havrincourt	24/11/1917	30/11/1917
Heading	War Diary 231st (Field) Company R.E. December 1917 Vol 19		
War Diary	Havrincourt	01/12/1917	03/12/1917
War Diary	Hamelincourt Croisilles	04/12/1917	26/12/1917
War Diary	Mory Ecoust	27/12/1917	31/12/1917
Heading	War Diary 231st (Field) Company R.E. January 1918 Vol 20		
War Diary	Mory Ecoust	01/01/1918	31/01/1918
Heading	War Diary 231st Field Coy R.E. February 1918 Vol 21		
War Diary	Mory Ecoust	01/02/1918	17/02/1918
War Diary	Croisilles	18/02/1918	28/02/1918
Heading	231st Field Company R.E. March 1918		
War Diary	Beinvillers Au-Bois	01/03/1918	10/03/1918
War Diary	Hamelincourt Boisleux (Armagh Camp)	10/03/1918	10/03/1918
War Diary	Armagh Camp (Boisleux-Hamelincourt Road)	11/03/1918	21/03/1918
War Diary	In Trenches opposite Hamelincourt Transport at Ayette	22/03/1918	22/03/1918
War Diary	In Trenches in Rear Of Behaginies Transport at Bucquoy	23/03/1918	25/03/1918
War Diary	Monchy Au. Bois	25/03/1918	25/03/1918
War Diary	Beinvillers Au-Bois	26/03/1918	26/03/1918
War Diary	Beinvillers	26/03/1918	26/03/1918
War Diary	Gouy En-Artois	27/03/1918	27/03/1918
War Diary	Sombrin	27/03/1918	28/03/1918
War Diary	Rocourt	29/03/1918	29/03/1918
War Diary	Sailly Sur. Lys-Fleurbaix	30/03/1918	30/03/1918
War Diary	B'Ac St Maur (Sailly)	31/03/1918	31/03/1918
Heading	231st Field Company R.E. April 1918		
Heading	War Diary 231st (Field) Company R.E. April 1918		
War Diary	Bac St Maur (Fleurbaix Sector)	01/04/1918	08/04/1918
War Diary	Bac St Maur	09/04/1918	09/04/1918
War Diary	Cul De Sac Farm	09/04/1918	09/04/1918
War Diary	Rue Pruvost (near Neuf Berquin)	10/04/1918	10/04/1918
War Diary	Le Verrier Steenwerck	10/04/1918	11/04/1918
War Diary	Strazeele Pradelles Road	11/04/1918	13/04/1918
War Diary	Maison Blanche	13/04/1918	13/04/1918
War Diary	Cormette	14/04/1918	20/04/1918
War Diary	Zutove	21/04/1918	22/04/1918

War Diary	St Sylvestre Cappel	23/04/1918	29/04/1918
War Diary	Cornhuyse (J.19.d. Central)	29/04/1918	30/04/1918
Heading	War Diary 231st (Field) Company R.E. May 1918 Vol 23		
War Diary	Cornyhuse	01/05/1918	31/05/1918
Heading	War Diary 231st (Field) Company R.E. June 1918 Volume 25		
War Diary	Cornhuyse	01/06/1918	08/06/1918
War Diary	Camp On Hondeghem Hazebrouck Road (V15a 5.1)	09/06/1918	30/06/1918
Heading	War Diary 231st (Field) Company R.E. July 1918 Volume 26		
War Diary	Camp on Hondeghem Hazebrouck Road V. 15. a. 5.1.	01/07/1918	31/07/1918
Heading	War Diary 231st (Field) Company, R.E. August, 1918		
War Diary	Camp on Hondeghem-Hazebrouck Rd V. 15.a. 5.1	01/08/1918	12/08/1918
War Diary	Camp-Hondeghem-Hazebrouck Rd (V15 a 5.1. Sheet 27)	13/08/1918	21/08/1918
War Diary	Camp Hondeghem Hazebrouck Rd	22/08/1918	22/08/1918
War Diary	Grass Camp (36 A/D9C 6.3)	23/08/1918	31/08/1918
Heading	War Diary 231st Field Company R.E. September 1918		
War Diary	Camp. 36A/D16b2.9	01/09/1918	15/09/1918
War Diary	Camp 36/A. A27. C. 22.	16/09/1918	25/09/1918
War Diary	Camp B7C 35.15 (Sheet 36 N.W.)	26/09/1918	30/09/1918
Heading	War Diary 231st (Field) Company, R.E. October 1918 Vol-29		
War Diary	Sheet 36 N.W.B.7C 35.15	01/10/1918	03/10/1918
War Diary	Sheet 36 N W B12b 4.4	03/10/1918	05/10/1918
War Diary	H 11a 5.3	06/10/1918	15/10/1918
War Diary	Nouvelle Houplines SL 36M. C27a 1.8	16/10/1918	16/10/1918
War Diary	36 NE/J1 B.77	17/10/1918	17/10/1918
War Diary	SH. 36 NE/J1b 7.7	17/10/1918	17/10/1918
War Diary	36 NE/D30a 7.7	18/10/1918	18/10/1918
War Diary	36 NE/F27b 9.9	19/10/1918	19/10/1918
War Diary	F27b 9.9	20/10/1918	20/10/1918
War Diary	Roubaix Area F 27b 9.9 (Sheet 36)	21/10/1918	25/10/1918
War Diary	Leers Nord Area H8 Central (Sheet 37)	26/10/1918	31/10/1918
Heading	War Diary 231st (Field) Company, R.E. November, 1918.		
War Diary	Leers Nord (H8 Central) Sheet 37	01/11/1918	08/11/1918
War Diary	Warcoing	09/11/1918	13/11/1918
Miscellaneous			
War Diary	La Madeline (36/K21C 3.3) 36/K29a 9.5)	26/11/1918	30/11/1918
Heading	War Diary 231st (Field) Coy. R.E. December 1918		
War Diary	St Maurice (Lille-36/K29a 9.5)	01/12/1918	26/12/1918
War Diary	36/K 29a 9.5	27/12/1918	31/12/1918
Heading	War Diary 231st (Field) Co. R.E. January 1919		
War Diary	St Maurice 36/K 29a. 9.5	01/01/1919	31/01/1919
Heading	War Diary. 231st Field Company. R.E. February 1919 Vol. 29.		
War Diary	St. Maurice. 36/K20a 9.5.	01/02/1918	31/03/1918
Heading	231 Fd Co. R.E. Mar 1919		

woos/2bo1/1

40TH DIVISION

231ST FIELD COY R.E.

JUN 1916 - MAR 1919.

~~From~~

To 3 DIV TROOPS

WAR DIARY
or
INTELLIGENCE SUMMARY
(Erase heading not required.)

Army Form C. 2118

231 F.C R.E
Vol 1

Place	Date	Hour	Summary of Events and Information	Remarks and references to Appendices
Blackdown	3/6/16	1pm	Re march out of the R.E Barracks Blackdown. Entrained (from tank RLWY) Station for Southampton where we embark	
Havre	4/6/16	8am	do. disembark & go up to N°5 Dock Rest Camp.	
Havre	5/6/16	6.30pm	Re entrain at point 6	
Lepig les Aire	6/6/16	5.30pm	Re we have after dis entraining at Berguette at 2.30 pm and marching the 8 miles	
"	7/6/16		Re Up and the day at Lepig les Aire	
Drouvin	8/6/16	3.30pm	Are we have from Lepig leaving 2nd Lt at Port & 1 N.C.O & 10 men to attend a demonstration of the styleantic Pipe Pusher at 10th	
Les Brebis	9/6/16	1pm	Re arrived here river tail into billets attached to the XXV. F.R Reid's, Clark & Barton & N.C.O 1 & 2 Sections having been detailed at Petit Sain Aux Bords rent to Calonne to do work with the XLIII Bg R.E	

WAR DIARY or INTELLIGENCE SUMMARY

Army Form C. 2118

Place	Date	Hour	Summary of Events and Information	Remarks and references to Appendices
Les Brebis	10/6/16		N⁰ˢ 1 & 2 Sections engaged on work at night - The support line at Calonne in deep dugouts under advice of X Rˢ. N⁰ˢ 3 & 4 Sections engaged in revetting the Maroc line between Maroc & Calonne under direction of X XVI Cy Rˢ. The Post Estaminets & his party atting the demolition j to Hy Chaulie Pipe Pushes at Bel Rene	
"	11/6/16		Sections all working as before. Lieut Postlethwaite returns by to Les Brebis	
"	12/6/16		Sections working as on 11th	
"	13/6/16 14/6/16 15/6/16		and 16th would the section of the Lakin to prepare deep dugouts	
	16/6/16		Sections working as on 12th	

WAR DIARY
or
INTELLIGENCE SUMMARY
(Erase heading not required.)

Army Form C. 2118

Place	Date	Hour	Summary of Events and Information	Remarks and references to Appendices
Les Brebis	17/6/16		At 4.30 pm a shell burst in billets occupied by No 4 section & killed Pioneer Scott & wounded 6 others.	
"	18/6/16		Sections working as before Nos 1 & 2 Calonne Nos 3 & 4 in village line & South E respectively	
"	19 & 20/6/16		Sections working ditto	
"	25/6/16		Church Parade 2.30 pm Rations ditto	
"	26/6/16		Sections working as usual as before	
"	27/6/16		Sapper Gill No 1 section X in A	
"	28/6/16		Sections as before	
"	29/6/16			
"	30/6/16		We move out at 2.0 pm to Division (La Bau Liette) take over own billets there	

J. McKenlor Lieut R.E. To O.C.
222nd Field Coy R.E. 1/7/16

40 July
231 F.R.E
Vol 2

War Diary
of
231st Field Company R.E.
40th Div

from 1st July 1916 to 31st July 1916.

WAR DIARY or INTELLIGENCE SUMMARY

Army Form C. 2118

(Erase heading not required.)

Instructions regarding War Diaries and Intelligence Summaries are contained in F.S. Regs., Part II. and the Staff Manual respectively. Title Pages will be prepared in manuscript.

Place	Date 1916	Hour	Summary of Events and Information	Remarks and references to Appendices
LA GAUCHETTE	1st July		Examination of billets - and thorough overhauling & inspection of kit & equipment and Transport.	J.D.
	2d "	10 A.M.	Church Parade. Orders received for move forward to take the place of the XXIII Company R.E.	J.D.
	3d "	11 A.M.	No. 3 Section march to LES BREBIS and then to CALONNE where they take over from a Section of the XXIII Company in Machine Gun Emplacements.	J.D.
	4th "	10 A.M.	Nos 1, 2, & 4 Sections march in to LES BREBIS and No 4 Section is detailed to CALONNE to take over work on the SUPPORT LINE. Nos 1 and 2 Sections take up quarters at LES BREBIS.	J.D.
LES BREBIS	5th "		No 4 Section - Support Line. No 3 Section M.G. Em. No 1 Section demolition wiring to Infantry parties & go out wiring at BOX TUNNEL. No 1 Section take up quarters at Calonne. No 2 Section on Brigade Work.	J.D.
	6th "		Nos. 3 & 4 Sections carry on work as before. 2 M.C.O.s + 24 men from each Bat.n in Brigade attack under No 1 Section in DEEP DUG OUTS. No 2 Section - work for Brigade and Company.	J.D.
	7th " 8th "		Work is started in shifts of 8 hours continuous on DEEP DUG OUTS. No 1 Section Superintending also instruction in wiring is given to Infantry parties. No 2 Section engaged on Bn. Brigade & Company work. Nos. 3 & 4 Sections as before.	J.D.
	9th "	1-30 A.M.	No 3 Section is heavily bombarded (T.M.s) L/Cpl. SMITH killed by Trench Mortar in Support Line.	J.D.
	10th "		Section No 1 DEEP DUG OUTS with attached miners Section 3 & 4 work in BOYAU THOMAS M.G.E. & BOX TUNNEL Section No 2. Brigade and Company work. Sand bag & timber supplies give out.	J.D.
	11th "		Telephone connection with LES BREBIS exchange made. O.C. and Lieut. Dowson survey the front line for support. No 1 Section detach a party of miners to work on the T.M. dugouts. No 1 section and remainder of miners continue work on the deep dug outs. No 2 Section Coy & Bdge work. No 3 Section M.G.E., Nos 5 & Nos 2. No 4 Section in BOYAU THOMAS and BOX TUNNEL - revetting & clearing.	J.D.

1875 Wt. W593/826 1,000,000 4/15 J.B.C. & A. A.D.S.S./Forms/C. 2118.

WAR DIARY
or
INTELLIGENCE SUMMARY
(Erase heading not required.)

Army Form C. 2118

Place	Date 1916	Hour	Summary of Events and Information	Remarks and references to Appendices
LES BREBIS	12th July		It is decided to make a tank of concrete to keep reserve of water for Calonne, and we obtain permission to proceed with the work.	JP
	13th July		No 2 Section go up to CALONNE. No 3 SECTION come to billets in LES BREBIS. No 1 Section working on DEEP DUG OUTS and T.M. Stores & Wiring. No 4 Section - Revetting SUPPORT LINE and loopholing traverses.	JP
			No 1 Section working continuously on HOXTON ROAD - 22b. DEEP DUG OUTS. TME at CRASSIER. 5 v ALY ALLEY. No. 2 Section make a start on M.G.Es and reconnoitring trenches etc. for future guidance. No 3 Section return to Calonne.	JP
	14th July	15 o'c	No 4 Section BOYAU THOMAS - BOYAU No 235: revetting. No 1 Section continue work as previously. Nos 2 & 3 Sections work together on M.G.Emp: The Water Cistern (CONCRETE) to hold a 2 days supply is put in hand - ground cleared etc. No 4 Section work as before.	JP
	15th July		It is decided to work the Sections in pairs :- 1 and 4: 2 and 3. Sections 1&4 take Deep Dug Outs & TME. Sections 2&3 take M.G.Emp. General.	JP
	16th July 17th July 18th July		As before	JP
	19th July		1 and 4 Section finish DUGOUT - BOYAU No 22b. 2&3 Sections as before.	JP
	20th July 21st July 22nd July		All Sections at work continuously. Instruction in Wiring given to Infantry.	JP
	23rd July		Lieut. E.J. Dowson and 3 N.C.Os from this Company proceed to the Gas School for 3 days course (HOUCHIN).	JP

WAR DIARY
or
INTELLIGENCE SUMMARY
(Erase heading not required.)

Army Form C. 2118

Place	Date 1916	Hour	Summary of Events and Information	Remarks and references to Appendices
LES BREBIS	23rd July.		A much larger front is allotted, and a great deal more supervision required:- Sections continue to work as before for the present. Headquarters Section are busy with Brigade and Company work, A large T.M. BASE is completed. Stables renovated. Range finder finished and Latrines constructed to M.O.s requirements. Paper Traps made for Brigadier.	J.D.
	24th July.		Sections working as usual, No 107294 Sapper Williamson. J. Wounded whilst working on Rifle Grenade	J.D.
	25th July.	2AM	No 107294 Sapper J. Williamson Died in Hospital (No 1 Clearing Station, CHOCQUES.)	J.D.
	26th "			
	27th "			
	28th "		Sections continue to work as before...	J.D.
	29th "			
	30th "			
	31st "			

J Rawes(?) Captn R.E.
2⅟⁴ Field Company

Vol 3

CONFIDENTIAL
WAR DIARY
of
231st (FIELD) COY RE
from Aug 1st 1916 to Aug 31st 1916

VOLUME 3

WAR DIARY
or
INTELLIGENCE SUMMARY

(Erase heading not required.)

AUGUST 1916   23rd FIELD COY RE 40th DIVISION

Army Form C. 2118

Place	Date	Hour	Summary of Events and Information	Remarks and references to Appendices
LES BREBIS	1 8/16		SECTIONS 1 and 4. Trench Mortar Emplacements at Calonne. HEADQUARTERS General repairs for Brigade. SECTIONS 2 . 3 Machine Gun Emplacements at Calonne and WATER CISTERN.	EgD
	2 8/16		Ditto. Improvement of billets scheme commenced.	EgD
	3 8/16		Private J.J. Swarbrick transferred from R.A.M.C. Minerour (Reinforcement) (Carpenter) Posted to No1 Section.	EgD
	4 8/16			EgD
	5 8/16		SECTIONS WORKING as before	
	6 8/16			
	7 8/16		SECTIONS as before. We are notified that Sap. McLeod No 14212 is posted to 231st Fd Coy RE from 12 2/16 at present being employed at No 1 Mobile Workshop BETHUNE.	EgD
	8 8/16			
	9 8/16			
	10 8/16			
	11 8/16		SECTIONS WORKING as before	
	12 8/16			
	13 8/16			
	14 8/16			
	15 8/16		10 (Ten) men received as reinforcements from BASE. LES BREBIS Shelled. 2 Drivers wounded - admitted to H.P. No 107, 291 Driver Pearson. W. and No 105, 406 Dr Gratrix. C. both Evacuated. Sections as before.	EgD
	16 8/16		PARTY of 1 Officer and 52 NCOs + Men attached for work on DUGOUTS in CALONNE.	EgD
	17 8/16		SECTIONS WORKING as before	
	18 8/16		231st Coy RE undertake supervision and give advice on Billet improvement at BULLY-GRENAY- GRENAY- CALONNE.	EgD

WAR DIARY
or
INTELLIGENCE SUMMARY
(Erase heading not required.)

Army Form C. 2118

Place	Date	Hour	Summary of Events and Information	Remarks and references to Appendices
LES BREBIS	19/7/16		Sapper Robinson EF No.144,566. Discharged from Hospital.	Egd.
	20/8/16			Egd.
	21/8/16		Water Cistern to Red S/400 fallow filled. — " —	Egd.
	22/8/16		——— SECTIONS WORKING as before ———	Egd.
	23/8/16		Sapper Lawlor discharged from Corps Rest Camp to duty. — " — Attached miners return to their respective Regiments in 119th Inf. Brigade.	Egd.
	24/7/16		10 Offrs and 104 N.C.Os +Men attached from 120th Brigade to replace 119th fowly returned.	Egd.
	25/8/16		Sections at work in Calonne as before. Headquarters on Improvement of Billets scheme, and General repairs...	Egd.
	26/8/16		Sections at work at CALONNE as before. News received and read on parade that Pioneer B.T. Hird had been awarded the Military Medal for action on 15th inst during	Egd.
	27/8/16		the shelling of LES BREBIS. Cpls H & J. Kennet, withdrew (eye wash)	Egd.
	28/8/16		Sections at work as before. General cleaning of billets and trenches for handing over to 63rd Div.	Egd.
	29/8/16	6 p.m.	Sections return from CALONNE. SECTIONS 3+4 proceed to MAROC. Nos 1+2 SECTIONS remain in billets in LES BREBIS.	Egd.
	30/8/16		General billet improvement, making 3 Tin trunks to accommodate extra 2 Sections.	Egd.
	31/8/16		" "	Egd.
			Mj.Brigade workshop commenced. 2 Sections in Maroc happen to S. Kennet evacuated to N.R. C.C.S.	Egd.

JaukDenpathaly I.R.E.
For OC 221st Field Coy R.E.

Army Form C. 2118

WAR DIARY
or
INTELLIGENCE SUMMARY
(Erase heading not required.)

Instructions regarding War Diaries and Intelligence Summaries are contained in F.S. Regs, Part II. and the Staff Manual respectively. Title Pages will be prepared in manuscript.

Place	Date	Hour	Summary of Events and Information	Remarks and references to Appendices
LES BREBIS	1.9.16.		SECTIONS 1 and 2 proceeded to MAROC to work on VILLAGE + RESERVE LINE. SECTIONS 3 and 4 working on Finchley Road + General Bilsi construction etc.	E.J.D.
	2			
	3			
	4			
	5		SECTIONS AT MAROC WORKING as previously.	E.J.D.
	6			
	7			
	8			
	9	10.30pm	Captain Reid-Kerr reported to commence 231st Field Coy. RE.	E.J.D.
	10		SECTIONS WORKING as before	
	11			E.J.D.
	12	12.30pm	Captain Reid-Kerr returned to 1st Indian Field Squad. RE. 1st Ind. Cavalry Div.	E.J.D.
			1 Lt. Turner G. detailed to attend Special works course at Special works farm R.E. WIMEREUX	
	13		Sections working as before.	E.J.D.
	14		" " " " Demonstration with Pipe Pushing Jack.	
	15	2/15pm	" " " " Sapper Kenny No.106670 returned from Hospital. (TEETH)	E.J.D.
	16		" " " " 1 N.C.O. + 7 men (Pipe Pushing Instruction) proceed to report to O/C 216 F.Co. for RE.	
	17			
	18		1 Lt. Irwin RAMC (attached MO) proceeded for duty to 3rd Divn. Sapper Bennett 16 R–	E.J.D.
	19		G.S.W. R⁺ Little finger.	
	20		Sections working as before.	
	21		Sapper Cairney C 107263 proceeds to 1st Army School of Instruction – COUDETTE-au-BOIS-aux (RQ. 10 + 05)	E.J.D.

1875 Wt. W593/826 1,000,000 4/15 J.B.C. & A. A.D.S.S./Forms/C. 2118.

Army Form C. 2118

WAR DIARY
or
INTELLIGENCE SUMMARY
(Erase heading not required.)

Instructions regarding War Diaries and Intelligence Summaries are contained in F. S. Regs, Part II. and the Staff Manual respectively. Title Pages will be prepared in manuscript.

Place	Date	Hour	Summary of Events and Information	Remarks and references to Appendices
LES BREBIS	21/10		Sections working as before.	E.J.D.
	22/10	4pm	Major Gillis 1/1st 105th Coys. taken to Hospital. Captain E.H. Johnson V.C. R.E. reported to command 231st 2d. Coy. R.E. (auth: 1st Army A/285/99 d/20/10) Company leave manor for — Sections 1 and 2 (1/4 Bis Sectn) "Forward Rivers" Sections 3 and 4 in PHILOSOPHE	E.J.D.
	23/10	7:15 AM	Sapper N. Wraith proceeded on Special leave. Reinforcement Beechwood Jnr. reported for duty.	E.J.D.
		3.15 pm	Capt. Truckett R.A.M.C. returned from LENS. Driver Collis no 105293 discharged from hospital.	
	24/10		Sapper Pearson E 107190 and Sapper Barnett J 116922 discharged from hospital.	E.J.D.
	25/10		Sapper Frost H. admitted to Hospital.	
	26/10		⎫	
	27/10		⎬ SECTIONS working same SECTOR as before	E.J.D.
	28/10		⎭ 14 BIS	
	29/10			
	30/10		Sections 1 and 2 (14 bis Sector) change with Sections 3 & 4 (PHILOSOPHE)	

O.C. 231st 2d Coy R.E.

Vol 5

CONFIDENTIAL.

War Diaries.

231st Field Company, R.E.

October, 1916.

VOLUME V

WAR DIARY or INTELLIGENCE SUMMARY

Army Form C. 2118

OCTOBER

Place	Date 1916	Hour	Summary of Events and Information	Remarks and references to Appendices
PHILOSOPHE + Lt BIS VILLAGE-LINE	Oct. 1		SECTIONS 1,2,3,4. at work on dugouts - Revetting - Clearing - etc. RAILWAY Repaired 15 Lt BIS. Sapper Wraith 106714 Returned from leave.	E.p.D.
	2nd			
	3rd		Sapper E. Smith 107136 to Hospital. Lieut. E.J. Dowson proceeded on leave to England. Sgr. Robinson. A 105390 and L/Cpl. Nicks T.W. 105,344 to Hospital for Dental Treatment.	E.p.D. E.p.D. E.p.D.
	4			
	5		SECTIONS at WORK as before	E.p.D.
	6		Sap. Wraith F. to Hospital. (106714)	E.p.D.
	7		Sapper Smith E. 107136 Returned to duty.	E.p.D.
	8		"	
	9		Movement of Company H.Q. from LES BREBIS To PHILOSOPHE. Sapper Wraith F. 106714 Ret from H. Coyt. Sapper Walker W. 155,653 reinforcement reported for duty from BASE. Sapper Robinson E.F. 161,1025 for Tech.	E.p.D. E.p.D. E.p.D.
	10		SECTIONS at WORK as before	E.p.D.
	11		Lieut E.J. Dowson returned from leave. Sapper Kenny 106690 to H.P. Company take over HULLUCH SECTOR - Nos 1 and 2 in the line Nos 3 and 4 section + H.Q. billeted PHILOSOPHE. Mounted Section + 11 Sappers remain at LES BREBIS.	E.p.D. E.p.D. E.p.D.
	12			
	13		SECTIONS at WORK as before	E.p.D.
	14			
	15			
	16		Rifle Wield A.A. 99262 killed in Action by Rifle Fire in front line. Sapper Champetier attached to 31st BrTh Coy. RE. for duty. (O.T)	E.p.D. E.p.D.

Army Form C. 2118

WAR DIARY
or
INTELLIGENCE SUMMARY
(Erase heading not required.)

Instructions regarding War Diaries and Intelligence Summaries are contained in F. S. Regs., Part II. and the Staff Manual respectively. Title Pages will be prepared in manuscript.

Place	Date 1916	Hour	Summary of Events and Information	Remarks and references to Appendices
PHILOSOPHE	17.10.		Sections 3 and 4 take over from Sections 1 and 2 at HULLUCH. Sapper Mallinder 107262 20 H.	EgB.
↓	18.10.		Sgt. Robinson A. 105,390. Cpl. Dicks T.W. 105,341. Returned from R. 15 July.	EgB.
VILLAGE LINE	19.10.			
	20.10.		140153 Sap. Landy reported for duty from 31st (A.T.) Coy. R.E.	EgB.
	21.10.		14,212 . McLeod DW joined company from Mobile Workshop, Bethune.	EgB.
	22.10.		107,352 . Bell E. 20 H. 107,271 Sap. Wailes J. rejoined Coy. from MINX. 107/136 Sap. Coleridge E.	EgB.
			144,549 Sap. Middleton rejoined Company from Bethune.	EgB.
	23.10.		rejoined Coy. from Bethune.	EgB.
			SECTIONS at WORK as before.	
	24.10.		All sections at PHILOSOPHE.	
	25.10.		Company leave PHILOSOPHE for LES BREBIS. (Sapper Shine 1R153 & 1915 H.)	EgB.
	26.10.		" " LES BREBIS for BRUAY.	EgB.
	27.10.		" " BRUAY for HOUVELIN. (Sapper Walsh A. 106714 H.)	EgB.
	28.10.		" " at HOUVELIN in Billets.	EgB.
	29.10.		" " " "	EgB.
	30.10.		" " " "	EgB.
	31.10.		" " " "	EgB.

EgBrown Capt.
Capt Commanding 23rd Field Coy R.E.

Confidential

WAR DIARY

231st Field Company R.E.

November, 1916

VOLUME VI

WAR DIARY or INTELLIGENCE SUMMARY

Army Form C. 2118

November 1916.

Place	Date	Hour	Summary of Events and Information	Remarks and references to Appendices
Houvelin	1.11.16		In billets	E.J.B.
Ocoche	2.11.16		Company left HOUVELIN arrived OCOCHE.	E.J.B.
	3.11.16		at Ocoche.	E.J.B.
Rougefay	4.11.16		left Ococho arrived ROUGEFAY.	E.J.B.
Montegny	5.11.16		left Rougefay - MONTEGNY.	E.J.B.
Dormart-En-Ponthieu	6.11.16		left Montegny - DORMART-EN-PONTHIEU.	E.J.B.
"	7.11.16		at DORMART EN PONTHIEU	E.J.B.
"	16	"	at work on V Army School.	E.J.B.
"	23.11.16	"	left DORMART arrived VAUCHELLES	E.J.B.
Vauchelles	24.11.16		at VAUCHELLES.	E.J.B.
	25.11.16		left VAUCHELLES arrived BUIGNY L'ABBE.	E.J.B.
Buigny L'Abbe	26.11.16		at work on Improvement of Billets for 119th Inf. Brigade.	E.J.B.
	28.11.16			E.J.B.
	30.11.16		No 2 Section Billeted at Pont Remy	E.J.B.

E.J. Boston Lt. R.E.
for o/c 2st Field Coy R.E.

Confidential

War Diary
of
231st Field Coy R.E.

December 1916. Volume VII

Army Form C. 2118

WAR DIARY or INTELLIGENCE SUMMARY

(Erase heading not required.)

231st Field Co. R.E. 4oth Division

DECEMBER 1916

Place	Date	Hour	Summary of Events and Information	Remarks and references to Appendices
BUIGNY L' ABBE	1.12.16		Sections at work in BUIGNY L'ABBE & district on improvements to Billets.	GHF
	7.12.16			GHF
	8.12.16		Mounted Section moved by road to SAILLY-LE-SEC. Company less Mounted Section march to Pont Remy & Entrain at 8 am. for MERRICOURT	GHF GHF
	9.12.16	12.30pm	Arrive at MERRICOURT L'ABBE, March to SAILLY LE SEC.	
		3.0pm	MOUNTED SECTION arrive by road.	GHF
SAILLY LE SEC.	10.12.16		COMPANY fitting & improving billets	GHF
	11.7.16		Sections 1, 2, 3, & 4 at work on improving Camps 12, 124, 125 at SAILLY LAURETTE & CHIPILLY.	GHF
	12.12.16			GHF
	13.12.16			
	14.12.16	8.30am	Sections 1 & 4 remove to billets on the work at Camp 12.	GHF
	15.12.16		" at work as before -	GHF
	16.12.16			GHF
	17.12.16	8.30am	Section 3 remove to Billets on work at Camp 111 near BRAY.	GHF
	18.12.16		Sections at work as before, Improving Camps.	GHF
	26.12.16			GHF
	26.12.16		Sections 1 & 4 rejoin Company at SAILLY-LE-SEC.	GHF
	27.12.16	9.30am	Company less No 3 Section move off for Camp 20 - where No 3 Section rejoin Company.	GHF
	28.12.16	9.30am	" MOVE to DOMINO DUMP.	GHF

(2)

Army Form C. 2118

WAR DIARY
or
INTELLIGENCE SUMMARY

(Erase heading not required.)

Instructions regarding War Diaries and Intelligence Summaries are contained in F. S. Regs., Part II. and the Staff Manual respectively. Title Pages will be prepared in manuscript.

December 1916.

Place	Date	Hour	Summary of Events and Information	Remarks and references to Appendices
DOMINO-DUMP	29/12/16		Sections at work on Splinter proofs, New horse lines, Rear Div HQ. Bath house, Sock drying sheds and Billet improvement.	
	30/12/16		Company at work as above	
	31/12/16			

B H Johnson
Major RE. D. Commanding
231st Field Coy. Royal Engineers.

Confidential

Vol 8

War Diary
of
231st Field Company R.E.

month of January 1917

VOLUME VIII

WAR DIARY
INTELLIGENCE SUMMARY

January 1917.

Army Form C. 2118

(i)

Place	Date	Hour	Summary of Events and Information	Remarks and references to Appendices
DOMINO DUMP Nr MAUREPAS B.15.b.2.4.	1917 January 1		Company at work as follows:— Divisional H.Q, Reg. Latrine, Dug Outs and Camp improvements Rear Divisional H.Q, Red Farm, Horse Lines, Bath House at MAUREPAS — Stables for BRIGADE. MOUNTED SECTION "TRANSPORT" at B.19 c.6.6. (b.2.c.N.W.)	H.C.
	2		Company at work as before. Brigade workshop started at B.15 b.2.4. with 12 Sappers from HQ 5th Inf. Bgde.	H.C.
	3		REINFORCEMENTS Two O.R. joined Company from Base.	H.C.
	4		2 Lieut POSTLETHWAITE and No. 106960 Sgt. N. Ogden (with Dr.?.Sears officers Batman) proceeded to 1st Army School for Course of Instruction.	H.C.
	5		Company at work as before.	H.C.
	6		"	H.C.
	7		"	H.C.
	8		ONE O.R. wounded in billets by Shrapnel at B.15 b.2.4. To H.P. 5th 7.	H.C.
	9			
	10			
	11			
	12		REINFORCEMENTS ONE O.R joined company from HQ 1st F.T.Co.R.E.	H.C.
	13			
	14			
	15			
	16		ONE O.R. TRANSFERRED to 153rd Fd. Co. 37th Divt. to join brother.	H.C.
	17		Company at work as before.	H.C.
	18		" " " 2/Lt G.C. SMYTH R.E. Posted to 231st F.C. RE " " " 2/Lt G. TURNER R.E. Transferred to Heavy Branch M.G. Corps. " " " Capt F.H. JOHNSON V.C.R.E. receives authority to rank as MAJOR.	H.C.
	19		2 O.R. REINFORCEMENTS joined Company from Base.	H.C.

WAR DIARY or INTELLIGENCE SUMMARY

Army Form C. 2118

January 1917. (ii)

(Erase heading not required.)

Place	Date	Hour	Summary of Events and Information	Remarks and references to Appendices
DOMINO DUMP B15.b.2.4.	January 19.		MAJOR F.H. JOHNSON. V.C. R.E. proceeds on course of R.E. instruction to R.E. School LE PARCQ (Dr WRACY, BETHUNE)	the
	20		" LIEUT G.C. SMYTH R.E. appointed Acting Adjut. Field Engr's. instructed to report to C.E. IVth Corps.	the the
	21		" LIEUT CLARKE assumes Command of Company in the absence of Major Johnson	the the
	22		Company at work as before	
	23		" " " "	the
	24		" " " " — 2/Cpl. R. Andrews proceeded to report to 1st Bn. Lincolnshire Regt. 21st Div. 1st Army.	
	25		" " " " —	the
	26		" " " " — " Lt. McBAIN reported for duty from Base	the the
	27		Company leave Domino Dump B15.b.2.H. and move to NISSEN HUTS at A30.b.6.H.	
	28		THREE SECTIONS WIRING at H.6.b+d. ONE SECTION on CAMP IMPROVEMENTS at A30.b.6.H.	the
	29		Company at work as before.	
	30			
	31			

F.W. Clarke Lieut R.E.
Actg. O/c 231st Field Coy.

Vol 9

CONFIDENTIAL. Vol 9

A.P.O. S 2118.

231st (Field) Company, R.E.

February 1917.

Army Form C. 2118

WAR DIARY
or
INTELLIGENCE SUMMARY

February 1917

(Erase heading not required.)

Place	Date	Hour	Summary of Events and Information	Remarks and references to Appendices
CAMP 101 A 30 b 6.4.	1.2.17		Company wiring Intermediate Line at H.Q. fords and Camp Improvements (XV Corps) under XV A. Boyles.	GHF
	to		Night work	GHF
Near CURLU	15		Day work.	GHF
	10.2.17			
	11.2.17		Company at work as above. Sapper Co. Reeton 107,312. wounded. Shrapnel enduty H.Bank.	GHF
	12.2.17		"	
	to		"	
	16.2.17		"	GHF
	17.2.17		Company wiring Road wood C.25.a.	
	18.2.17		"	
	to		"	
	23.2.17		"	GHF
	24.2.17		½ Company wiring at C.8.b (Night) under 10th Div.?	GHF
	25.2.17		" " " Sapper Asquith J. wounded Shrapnel on duty C.8.b.	
	26.2.17		" " "	GHF
	to		" " " Sapper Gibson J. wounded Shrapnel on duty C.8.b	
	28.2.17		" acting "	GHF
x	14.2.17		Lt. Clark to be Captain (War 121 d/62m)	RE

A. Johnson
Major RE

Vol 10

CONFIDENTIAL

231st Field Company R.E.

WAR DIARIES

Vol 10

WAR DIARY or INTELLIGENCE SUMMARY

(Erase heading not required.)

March 1917

Army Form C. 2118

231st FIELD Coy RE 40TH DIV

Place	Date	Hour	Summary of Events and Information	Remarks and references to Appendices
CAMP 161 A.30.B.6.4. NEAR CURLU	1-3-17 to 16		Company night wiring at C.8.b. under XVth Corps and Camp Improvements by day work	JH
	5-3-17		Sections move to B.30.c.5.5. Transport to H.13.a.3.5.	JH
	6-3-17		3.O.R. REINFORCEMENTS joined Coy from Base. No 1 Section laying metals to Aid Post c. 25.6.6.9. Nos 2 + 3 making dug outs.	JH
	7-3-17		Nos 2 + 3 making dug outs. Nort. Improvements to H.Q. dug outs. Coy. at work as before.	JH
	8-3-17		2nd Cpl. Stocks wounded at duty C.13.C.	JH
	9-3-17		Nos 1, 2 + 3 Sections on Dug.outs. No 4 Section as before.	JH
	10.3.17		Coy at work as top	JH
	11.3.17		" " "	JH
	12.3.17		2.0.P. REINFORCEMENTS joined Coy.	JH
	13.3.17		Coy. at work as before.	JH
	14.3.17		" " "	JH
	15.3.17		Company wiring Intermediate Line c. 25.a. Strong Point c.20.b. Making dug outs at c.19.d.7.1. c.20.R.4.5. Gun Position at B.30.c.6.5.	JH
	16.3.17		Coy. at work as before. No 1 Section move to B.30.b. central. LITTLEDALE	JH
	17.3.17		Company move to B.30.b. central LITTLEDALE BARRACKS. Transport remain at H.13.a.3.5. Sections at work as above.	JH
	18.3.17		Nos 2, 3, + 4 Sections repairing Roads from c.20.d. 21.6. c. 26. b.5.0. No 1 Section making Gun Post D.lore.	JH
	19.3.17		Company at work as before	JH
	20.3.17		No 3 Section move to I.4.a.8.8. No Section revetting channel for flow of TORTILLE RIVER. No 2 rd Section repairing BETHUNE ROAD.	JH

Army Form C. 2118

WAR DIARY
or
INTELLIGENCE SUMMARY
(Erase heading not required.)

March 1917

Place	Date	Hour	Summary of Events and Information	Remarks and references to Appendices
LITTLEDALE			231st FIELD Co. R.E. 40TH DIV	
	21.3.17		No 3 Section move to ALLAINES. Making Roads H.Q at I.4.C.8.4. Nos. 2.3. r 4	
	22.3.17		Sections road repairing	
			Transport move to ALLAINES. Company at work as before	
	23.3.17		Remainder of the Company move to ALLAINES. Section road repairing. " LIEUT. WILBURN posted with H.Q to 3rd Sect R.E. to take over the duties of Adjutant.	
	24.3.17		Company at work as before	
	25.3.17		Company move to LITTLEDALE BARRACKS. B.30.C. 6.O.R. REINFORCEMENTS joined Coy from Base	
	26.3.17		Sections road repairing c.15. b. 6. 4. c.16.a. 9.4. c.20 a.18. to c.8.a.5.1. c.16.a.9.4 to c.17.b.2.7. c.20.a.9.8 c.15.a.9.1.	
	27.3.17		Sections road repairing c.15.b.6.5. c.16 a 9.5. c.20.d.9. c.20 d.3.1. c.16. a. 9.5 to c.17 a.1.5. c.20.a.8.9. c.15.b.6.3. 7.O.R. REINFORCEMENTS joined Coy.	
	28.3.17		Sections road repairing c.15. b.6.3. c.16 a.9.5. c.18.a.8.4 D.7.d.9.2 c.16. a. 9.5. c.17.a.1.5. c.20.d.1.9 c.20.a. 3.1. " LIEUT MERRYLEES & C.S.M STEAD (work for LEE Officer) Batman proceed to ARMY SCHOOL for COURSE of INSTRUCTION	
	29.3.17		Sections at work as before.	
	30.3.17		"	
	31.3.17		"	

Vol XI

CONFIDENTIAL

—WAR DIARY—

Vol. XI

—231ˢᵗ (Field) Company R.E.—

April 1917

WAR DIARY or INTELLIGENCE SUMMARY

Army Form C. 2118

APRIL 1917

Place	Date	Hour	Summary of Events and Information	Remarks and references to Appendices
LITTLEDALE BARRACKS B.30.b.	1.4.17		Sections road making. 3.O.R. Join Company as Reinforcements. 107296 Sapper PEARSON. E. evacuated to 48. C.C.S. 11 Lieut PASTLETHWAITE to 56 Light from 27 det/16. Gazette 31·3·17.	
	2-4-17		Sections at work as before. 67252 Pnr SMALL A. evacuated to 48·C.C.S.	
	3-4-17		" " 2.O.R. Join Coy as Reinforcements	
	4-4-17		" " " "	
	5-4-17		" " " "	
ETRICOURT	6-4-17		COMPANY MOVE TO ETRICOURT. 3 SECTIONS working on Div. H.Q. at MANANCOURT.	
	7.4.17		1 SECTION dismantling GERMAN TRESTLE BRIDGE at V.2.d.2.2. 3 Sections as before 11 Lieut. WILBURN returns to Coy from Div. R.E. H.Q. Effective strength of Coy. 7 Officer 221 O.R. Attached 10.O.R.	
	8-4-17		Working on TRESTLE BRIDGE. ERECTING NISSEN HUTS at MANANCOURT for Div. H.Q.	
	9·4·17 10·4·17		Company at work as before	
	12-4-17		Setting out Line of Resistance YTRES - SOREL from W.7.c.4.9. Working on TRESTLES BRIDGE + erecting NISSEN HUTS. 179765 Sap. HAMMOND R. evacuated to N°5·C.C.S	
	13-4-17		Complete TRESTLE BRIDGE except for hand roadbearers. Working on Div. H.Q. Line of Resistance YTRES - SOREL. Week at ECOLE, ETRICOURT for Barks. 10665·8 Sap. FIELDSEND H. transferred to H.Q. 4th Army for duty with C.E.	
	14.4.17		Company at work as before. Effective strength of Coy. 7 Officers. 220. O.R. Attached 9.O.R.	
	15.4.17		Company at work as before 3.O.R Join Coy as Reinforcements	
	16.4.17		161.O.R - 2 Officers of the 119th Infantry Bgde Works Coy are attached to Coy for duty	
	17.4.17		Bridge completed for 3 ton lorry traffic. on Div. Barks at ETRICOURT on S-Y line	
	18.4.17		Company working on Div. Baths, ETRICOURT, also on YTRES - SOREL line of Resistance	

Army Form C. 2118

WAR DIARY
or
INTELLIGENCE SUMMARY

(Erase heading not required.)

APRIL
1917

Instructions regarding War Diaries and Intelligence Summaries are contained in F. S. Regs., Part II. and the Staff Manual respectively. Title Pages will be prepared in manuscript.

Place	Date	Hour	Summary of Events and Information	Remarks and references to Appendices
ETRICOURT.	19.4.17 / 20		Working on Div. Baths ETRICOURT & YTRE-SORBL. Line of Resistance Nº 4 SECTION	
	21.4.17		Move to EQUANCOURT to work under 229th FIELD Coy. R.E. Effective strength of Coy. 7 officers 221. O.R. Attached 2 officers 170 O.R.	
	22.4.17 / 23		Company at work as before.	
	24.4.17			
	25.4.17		2. O.R. Join Company as reinforcements, one section working on communication at Q.23.a.r.c. Remainder of Coy. as before.	
	26.4.17		2 sections working on communication trench at Q.23.a.r.c. One section working on Baths.	
	27.4.17		2 sections move to W.2.a.9.1. Company at work as before	
	28.4.17		Completed Div. Baths. Remainder of Coy at work as before. Attached Infantry move to new billets near DESSART WOOD. Effective strength of Coy. 7 officers 220. O.R. Attached = 2 officers 176 O.R.	
	29.4.17		Nº 4 SECTION returned to Coy. H.Q at ETRICOURT.	
	30.4.17		Nº 4 SECTION moved to new billets about W.2.a.9.1.	

H. Johnson
Major. R.E.

WAR DIARY
or
INTELLIGENCE SUMMARY
(Erase heading not required.)

Army Form C. 2118

Instructions regarding War Diaries and Intelligence Summaries are contained in F. S. Regs., Part II. and the Staff Manual respectively. Title Pages will be prepared in manuscript.

Place	Date	Hour	Summary of Events and Information	Remarks and references to Appendices
ETRICOURT.	8.4.17	—	*Details as to bridge erected.*	
	9.4.17		[Sketch of trestle bridge with dimensions 107'-6", 18'-0", 2' decking, and type of trestle showing 9"x9", 7"x7", 57"]	

Material for trestle were obtained from Rail Head Bridge 200 away. Material for super[structure] obtained partly from [illegible] at ETRICOURT. Trestles & [illegible] were built by men of a [illegible] [illegible] were hoisted [illegible] [illegible] on them to hold [illegible]. The abutments [illegible] [illegible] moving [illegible] the 2750 men having Bridge was [illegible] [illegible] [illegible] [illegible] [illegible] [illegible] [illegible] with [illegible] convoyed to carry 13 ton lorries by [illegible] [illegible] [illegible] [illegible] [illegible] by inserting additional crossbearers & rails, so to [illegible] [illegible] [illegible] [illegible] was [illegible] laterally by two A frames one on each end and against the centre trestle as shown in sketch.

G. Johnson
Major R.E.

CONFIDENTIAL

231st Field Co. R.E.

War Diary

From 1st May 1917
To 31st May 1917

Volume 12

WAR DIARY or INTELLIGENCE SUMMARY

Army Form C. 2118

MAY 1917

Place	Date May	Hour	Summary of Events and Information	Remarks and references to Appendices
DESSART WOOD	1st		O.C. and Nos 2, 3 & 4 sections in huts & shelters in DESSART WOOD (57°) No.1 Section moved to huts at EQUANCOURT. H.Q. & transport horse lines remained at ETRICOURT. No.1 Section erecting huts re-for Bgde H.Q. No. 2 & 3 erecting elephant shelters for Dmnd Ranging section near GOUZEAUCOURT laying & digging Maretz. No. 4 section on Batt? H.Q. in FIFTEEN RAVINE. New communications & remainder recd. & food by the SAP THORP wounded shrapnel	A/1
	2nd		As above. Sapr ROGER J. wounded & left for C.C.M. 97 BAD injured from US Army school	
	3rd 4th		As above No 2 section wiring at Q.16.6. - Q.18.d.	
	5th 6th		No Section wiring at R.14.b.8.6. As above. No.3 Section wiring at Q.18. Explosive charge of Coy ? Officer 217.O.R. attached 2 officers 178.O.R. Raid on 45 VACQUERIE carried out by two Brigades of 40th Division Party of R.E (2 Officers. 20 O. Ranks) & Officer & 16 attached infantry) accompany party of 20th Middlesex. R.E. failed to enter the village owing to accounting infantry being held up by enemy barrage. 2 P.R. MERRYLEES Officers NOBLE E., HILL R.E. OSBORN H. (at duty) Pr. MULLINS T (at duty) Pr. TAYLOR A & L/Cpl. WRACKAM. wounded by shell fire.	A/1
	7th		No 1 Section working on shelters for advanced Brigade H.Q. at 29 & Q.3.c. No. 2 section wiring at Q.16.b. No. 3 do do No. 4 do No. 29466 Pte. WRENCH R. Killed. No. 39274 Pte. BINNS A. No 453129 Pte. LEES E.H. No. 457730 Pte. RESANT (A.C0.19th R.W.F. attached & Coy) wounded by explosion of enemy premiums in salvage dump	A/1
	8th		No. 1 & 2 Sections as above. No 3 section shellering & letting out BROWN LINE (Intermediate Line) No. 4 Section traversing drawing front line approx R.14 & R.15.a (57.c.s.s. 20,000)	A/1
	9th		No.1 Section moved to Q.3.a.5.2. Wiring Brown Line at Q.16.b. Brown Line at Q.32.a.2.4. Wiring Brown Line Q.28.&.14.&.3 sheltering, harrowing drawing front lines at R.14.&.6.6.	A/1
	10th 11th		Company wiring at R.14.6. Brown Line Q.28.6. Sapr STOTHARD E. No. 179476 wounded by shell fire at Q.30.d.2.5. Evacuated to 55th C.C.S.	A/1

WAR DIARY or INTELLIGENCE SUMMARY

Army Form C. 2118

MAY 1917 (ii)

Place	Date MAY	Hour	Summary of Events and Information	Remarks and references to Appendices
DESSART WOOD	12		Wiring at R.14.c. - R.8.b. Spotlocking at R.14.c. Effective strength of Coy 6 Officers 215.O.R. attached 2 officers 170.O.R.	Aff
HEUDICOURT	13		Company move from DESSART WOOD to HEUDICOURT W.21.a.4.9. Transport from ETRICOURT to W.21.a.4.9. at work as before. Improving billets at HEUDICOURT.	Aff
	14		Working on Left. Bgde H.Q. X.3.d.6.3. Right Bgde H.Q. X.9.d.4.3.	Aff
	15		Drawing front line at X.7.b., digging dead Kent at X.11.c.	Aff
	16		Lieut D.E.KNIGHT reported for duty. 5.O.R. reinforcements from Base. Company working on H.Q. 121 Bgde. I. Making Southern HEUDICOURT - drawing front line & digging dead as above.	Aff
	17			Aff
	18		do. Effective strength of Coy 7 officers. 218.O.R. attached. 2 officers. 168.O.R.	Aff
	19		Drawing and deepening front line. 3.O.R. joined Coy. as reinforcements	Aff
	20		Preparing bangalores for minor enterprise. Wiring at X.16.	Aff
	21		Horse Lines at FINS. 11 Sappers take part in minor enterprise. Wiring at X.16. 3 holes, 2 p/ps, successful.	Aff
	22		Company move back to DESSART WOOD. W.2.a.9.1. Transport to FINS. V.11.d. central. 1.O.R. joined Coy. as Reinforcement.	Aff
DESSART WOOD	23		Wiring at X.16. & drawing front line. Drawing C.T. X.16.C.	Aff
	24		2 section making advanced billets at Q.34.c.7.8. 2 sections improving accomodation DESSART WOOD	Aff
	25		Company at work as above.	Aff
	26		At work as above. 1 section at work at Horse Lines W.7.c.3.6. Effective strength of Coy. 7 officers 222.O.R. attached 2 officers 168.O.R.	Aff
	27		Spotlocking at R.7.d.7.8. Bringing C.T. at R.14.C.7.8. Spotlocking communication in R.14.C. from R.14.d.2.8 to R.14.d.9.9. Digging C.T. from R.7.d.4.3 towards R.13.a.2.4	Aff
	28		Drawing C.T. from R.14. & R.7.d.9.9. from Billets 3.O.R. join Coy. at R.14. +	Aff
	29		No 3 Section move to new billets Q.34.c.4.8. from R.14.d.2.8. to new billets 3.O.R. join Coy as Reinforcement. Spotlocking C.T. from R.7.d.2.0 from R.7.d.2.0	Aff

Army Form C. 2118

WAR DIARY
or
INTELLIGENCE SUMMARY
(Erase heading not required.)

MAY 1917

Place	Date	Hour	Summary of Events and Information	Remarks and references to Appendices
DESSART WOOD	MAY 30 31		Improving my water point at R.13.d.4.9. Chitecking my C.T. line long improvement Estab established at R.2.c.8.6., R.9.6.80.15, R.8.c.39. Finished food and in front.	

J.H. Johnson
Major R.E.

WAR DIARY or INTELLIGENCE SUMMARY

Army Form C. 2118

JUNE (1)

Place	Date June	Hour	Summary of Events and Information	Remarks and references to Appendices
DESSART WOOD	1st		Company at work on new water point at R.13.0.4.9. and shotlocking gaps between front line posts. Aid Post at R.14.C.2.2.	
	2nd		Coy. at work as above No 146322 Sapper TAYLOR. E. wounded by shrapnel at R.14.A.3.2. No 107279 Sapper GIBSON.T. evacuated to No 41 Stationary Hospital.	
	3rd		Effective strength of Coy, 7 officers, 224. O.R. attached 2 officers 169 O.R. Company working at Coy Headquarters at R.8.c.7.3. Sapping through railway at R.8.c.7.7. Shelters in front line R.14.b central, water point at R.13.d.4.9. Shelter for M.G. position at R.14.a.3.2.	
	4th		Brigade relief.	
	5th		Company at work on sapping through railway at R.8.c.6.5. Also gun position at R.8.c.7.3. Front line shelters at R.14.B.6.4. Water point at R.13.d.H.9.	
	6th		No above. And Brigade bomb store at Q.29.a.6.4.	
	7th		At work as above. No 107136 Sapper SMITH. E. wounded (at duty) by shrapnel.	
	8th		At work as above.	
	9th		Company at work on Aid Post at R.13.6.8.1. Wiring front of posts at R.8.c.4.3. No 2. Section moved from forward billets to DESSART WOOD. Attached Infantry No 295743 Pt HUMPHRIES. A 18th Welsh Regt. KILLED. No 24175 Pt GALLOWAY J. No 35372 Pt LEWIS. W. No 23887 Pt WATSON. H No 23891 Pt WARDEN.W. all 12th S.W.B. wounded by hostile shell fire. No 107279. Sap. MARSDEN. L.M. transferred to H.Q. 140th Div R.E.
Effective strength of Coy 7 officers 219 O.R. attached 2 officers 158 O.R.	
	10th		Coy. at work as above.	
	11th		Coy. at work as above. No 144561. L.Cpl. WOOD. J.W. wounded (at duty) No 105193 Sapper PHIL. W.J No 160771 Sapper ROGERS. S. wounded by hostile shell fire at R.14.a.7.8.	

WAR DIARY or INTELLIGENCE SUMMARY

Army Form C. 2118

Place	Date JUNE	Hour	Summary of Events and Information	Remarks and references to Appendices
DESSART WOOD	12th		Company at work on Obs Post at 13.b.6.1. Brigade bomb store at R.19.a.9.5. Well and water storage VILLERS PLOUICH. R.13.b.4.9. Machine gun shelter at R.19.a.9.6. No. 144676 Sapper BREARLEY W. attached 40th Div Employment Coy. (Labour Corps).	JH
	13th		Coy at work as above.	JH
	14th		" " " Laying out new communication trench from new front line	JH
	15th		to support line N.R.8.a. (F.C.) Coy at work as above. No. 105781 Pnr HILL G.H. attached Infantry. No. 35727 L.Cpl. KING.W. No. 24028 Pte GIBBONS F. both 12th S.W.B. Killed. No. 24809 Pte SMITH A. No. 24438 Pte GODDARD.F. No. 23731 Pte KIDD J. No. 35506 Pte BURROWS.K. all 12th S.W.B. wounded by hostile shell fire at R.M. Central. No. 23687 Pte DORRINGTON'S 12th S.W.B. shell shock.	JH
	16th		Coy at work as above, & wiring in front of new front line R.8.a and R.14.b. Effective strength 9 officers 214 O.R. attached 2 officers 149 O.R.	JH
	17th		Coy at work as above. + Bathing point at R.2.c.2.0. No. 120975 Sgt DOYLE M. wounded by machine gun fire at R.8.a.	JH
	18th		Coy at work as above	JH
	19th		" " " "	JH
	20th		" " " "	JH
	21st		" " " " Aid post completed	JH
	22nd		Coy at work on front line shelter at R.14.b.6.3. Bringing trench at R.19.b.5.1. Drawing C.T. R.9.d.9.4. to R.9.b.9.1. Bathing point at R.2.a.2.0. Making cable trench for 40th Div. Signal Coy. Attached to Coy from 120th Brigade 44.O.R. for wiring instructions.	JH
	23rd		Drawing and laying trench boards in C.T. from old to new front line R.9.d.9.4. to R.9.b.9.1. Netting laid down in barricaded trench R.14.c.8.9. Well water storage R.13.b.4.0.	JH

WAR DIARY
INTELLIGENCE SUMMARY

Army Form C. 2118

JUNE (III)

Place	Date	Hour	Summary of Events and Information	Remarks and references to Appendices
DESSART WOOD	23rd		Making accommodation for area Commandant at DESSART WOOD. Effective strength of Coy. 7 Officers 213 O.R. attached 2 Officers 192 O.R.	
	24th		Coy at work as above	
	25th		— " —	
	26th		Deepening front line at R.7.b.6.2. Laying tunnel boards draining C.T. at R.7.a. boring at R.14.b.6.6. Well & water storage at R.13.d.4.7. Making accommodation for area Commandant at DESSART WOOD. One Saffr. & 3 O.R. Works Coy. attached to R.S.M. at TYKE DUMP. 4 NCO's from 120th Brigade attached for wiring instruction.	
	27th		Coy. at work as above. No 167641 Sapper HORST.H. & No 183987 Sapper FRANCIS E.M. wounded by hostile trench mortar at R.14.b. 65.55. No 145720 Pte WARD J & No 28435 Pte HERBERT T. both 19th R.W.F's wounded by machine gun fire at R.14.b.	
	28th		Battalion relief. Front line shelters at R.14.b. Well & water storage at R.13.d.4.7. Bench works at R.19.b.5.2. Making accommodation for area Commandant at DESSART WOOD.	
	29th		Trench boarding & draining C.T. at R.7.a. boring at R.14.b.8.5. Fixing pump at R.13.d.4.7.	
	30th			

Vol 14

Confidential
War Diary
231 Field Co RE
July 1917

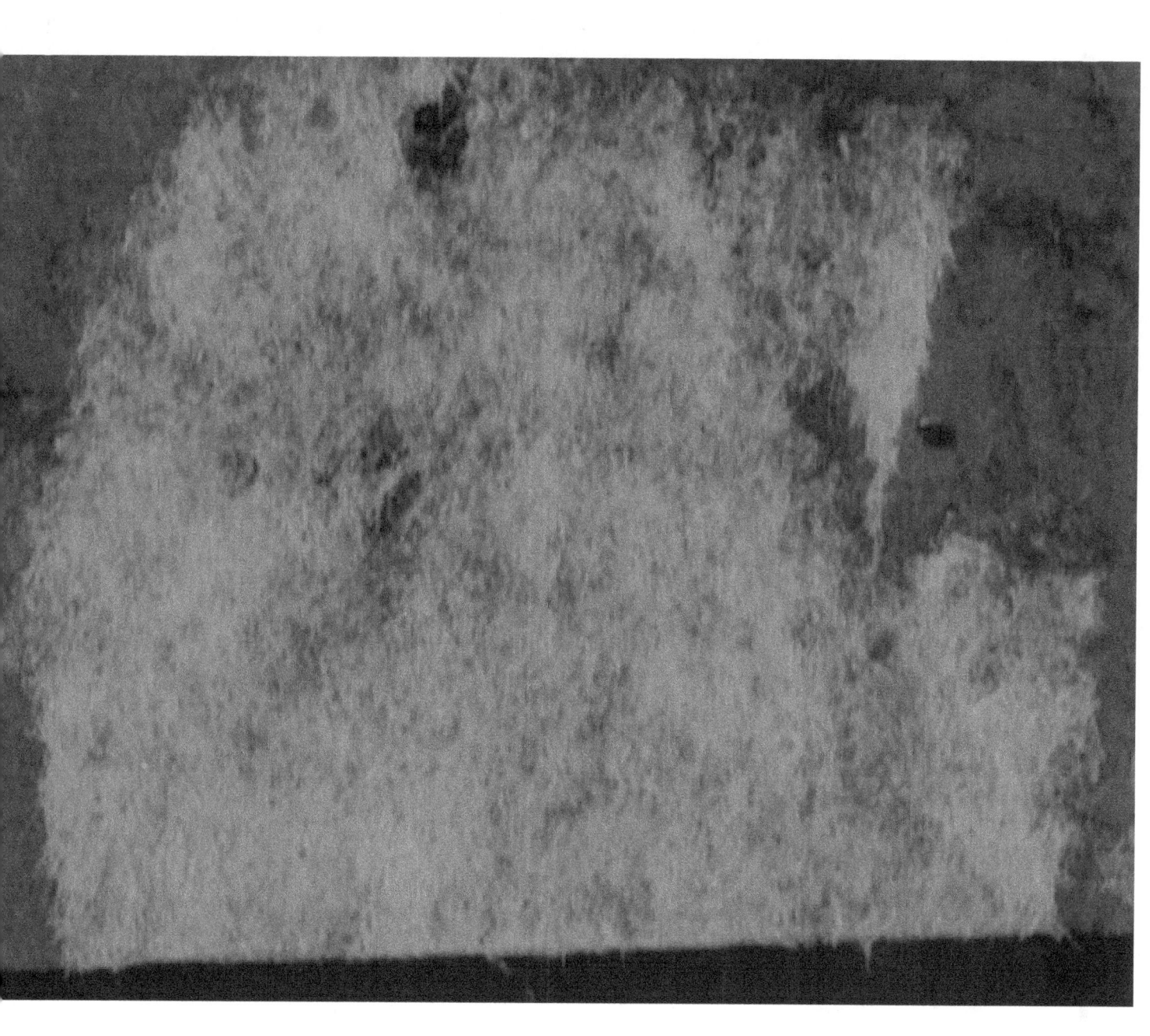

WAR DIARY

INTELLIGENCE SUMMARY

(Erase heading not required.)

JULY 1917
(1.)

Army Form C. 2118

Place	Date July	Hour	Summary of Events and Information	Remarks and references to Appendices
DESSART WOOD	1st		Not referred to throughout S.O.S.E. Lyon. Company at work draining and trench boarding C.T. in R.7.a. & R.14.a.37, hats permit at R.13.d.4.7. Trench bridge at R.19.b.5.2. Attached infantry working in C.T. R.7.a.	Off.
	2nd		Company at work, Trenchboarding front line at R.S.C. and draining C.T. at R.7.a. Trench boarding at R.14.a.4.8. Fitting up engine room and laying water main at R.13.a.4.7. Fitting up theatre at FINS and Bomb store at R.2.a.9.1. No 564.91. Sapper CROSS. A. transferred to R.E. Base, Rouen, no reinforcement for Acetch light Coy.	Off.
	3rd		Coy. at work as above. Attached Infantry spitlocking trench at R.14.a.7.5.	Off.
	4th		Coy. at work as above, and completing Japanese Baths at W.2.c.c.o. attached duty. Laying trench mats in R.14.a. No. 107795. Sapper ATKINSON.T. + No 107247. Sapper R.M.1b.3/4. attached duty 120th Bde. wiring party, No 30791 OSBORN.W. wounded by rifle fire. Pte. ASHDOWN. H. 14th H.L.I. killed in action, No 297690 Pte. STEWART.J. No 298091 Pte. GOW.P. wounded by machine gun fire.	Off.
	5th		Coy. at work as above. Att. Infy. spitlocking trench R.14.a. and carrying trench boards to R.14.a.	Off.
	6th		Coy. at work trench boarding CTs at R.14.a. and R.14.a.2.8. Bathing in huts forward billets at Q.30.b.1.9. Baths at W.9.a.4.7. Installing road to A.R.P. in W.3.a. Att. Infy. installing road to A.R.P. W.3.a.	Off.
	7th		Coy. at work laying trench boards at R.13.b. and R.14.a.2.8. Water point at R.13.a.4.7. Att. Infy. working on Road to A.R.P. W.3.a. and laying trench boards at R.14.a. No 3 Section above to DESSART WOOD. 208 O.R. attached 4 Officers 229 O.R. Officers strength 9 Officers	Off.

WAR DIARY or **INTELLIGENCE SUMMARY**

Army Form C. 2118

JULY 1919 (11)

Place	Date July	Hour	Summary of Events and Information	Remarks and references to Appendices
DESSART WOOD.	8th		Coy at work on new forward billets, Water point at R.M.a.b.9. Boring at R.M.a., Water point at R.13.a.4.9. Taping out new line R.M.a.b.9. Off duty working on road to A.R.S. R.2.a. Laying trench mats at R.13.B.	Off
	9th		Coy at work on new advance billets, Machine gun emplacements and shelters at R.26.b.3.7. Fixing pump at R.13.a.4.9. Laying trench mats at R.14.b.5. Off duty rigging C.T at R.13.b. and on new advanced billets.	Off
	10th 11th		Company and attached Infantry at work as above.	Off
			Coy at work as above and on C.T. to MOUNTAIN ASH TRENCH R.8.a. new C.T. in wood R.7.a.9.3. Rigging new front line R.m.d.6.4. Off duty laying trench boards R.19.b. and working on new C.T. R.7.9.a.	Off
	12th		Company and attached Infantry at work as above.	Off
	13th		Coy at work on new advanced billets R.30.b.1.9. Machine gun emplacements and shelters in R.26.b.37. Water point at VILLERS PLOUICH R.13.a.5.9. Fixing trench boards in POPE AVENUE. Attached duty laying trench boards.	Off
	14th		Coy and attached Infy. at work as above. 1 Officer strength 7 Officers 206 O.R. – attached 2 Officers 239 O.R.	Off
	15th		At work as above laying trench boards in TAFF VALE and DICK AVENUE, making extension of trench to "61st" Avenue through woods and railway R.8.C.7.9. Wiring new front line R.14.b.7.5. Laying trench boards R.14.C.7.8. Att. duty laying trench boards R.8.C, R.13.a. and R.19.b.	Off
	16th		At work as above. No 106848 Pioneer CLARK H. joined Company as Reinforcement. No.1 Section moved to new advanced billets Q.30.B.1.9	Off

WAR DIARY
INTELLIGENCE SUMMARY
(Erase heading not required.)

Army Form C. 2118

JULY 1917 (III)

Instructions regarding War Diaries and Intelligence Summaries are contained in F.S. Regs., Part II. and the Staff Manual respectively. Title Pages will be prepared in manuscript.

Place	Date	Hour	Summary of Events and Information	Remarks and references to Appendices
DESSART WOOD	17th		Coy at work as above. 406934 Sapper HARRIS.F.B. joined Company from 1"/N°2. Reinforcement Company	Off
	18th		Coy at work as above.	Off
	19th		Coy at work as above and no. 1 advanced billets at Q.30.b.1.9. Camouflage revewing to road W.3 central. MERTHYR TRENCH and cutting through road R.9.7.9 deepening trench and drains MOUNTAIN ASH TRENCH and C.T. to same R.8.A.15." BHQ shelters at R.13a.7.9. New RHONDDA TRENCH and laying french boards R.14 to 6.4.7 Wiring and digging new forward line R.14.A. Travel boarding R.7.a. Attached duty laying trench boards in TAFF VALE AVENUE and in C.T. in R.7.a.	Off
	20th		at work as above.	Off
	21st		at work as above. Company forward billets Q.30.b. Crupeites, Attached duty trench boarding R.7.d. R.13.a. & R.8.a. R.14.b. Effective strength 7 Officers 208 O.R. attached 3 Officers 223 O.R.	Off
	22nd		Batt. relief:- Revewing road at Q.29.B.2.0. Tactical wire at R.19 B.O.3. Shelters for B.H.Q. R.13 b. 7.9. Laying trench boards at R.14.b.3.3. N°2 Section moved to new forward billets R.30.B. N°4 Section moved to DESSART WOOD. No.1 Section take over work from No.3 Section. Shelter for B.H.Q TAFF VALE AVENUE	Off
	23rd		R.13 a. 7.9. deepening MERTHYR TRENCH R.8.C.5.7 Wiring at R.4.A. Attd Infantry R.7.d. + R.8.d. Trenchboarding on C.T. in R.7.d.	Off
	24th		Coy at work on C.T. across road at R.13 b. 7.5. C.T. through road R.14.a.5.3. Accommodation for Coy H.Q. at DANCIM RAVINE. Tactical wire at R.19a 6.5. att'd Infantry road repairing at R.25 + Q.36. Revewing road at 6.3 central. Deepening TAFF VALE AVENUE. 120th Inf Bde. Wiring party reforms their respective battalions	Off

1875 Wt. W503/826 f.oop.ooo 2/15 J.B.C.f & A. A.D.S.S. /Forms/C. 2118.

WAR DIARY
INTELLIGENCE SUMMARY
(Erase heading not required.)

Army Form C. 2118

JULY 1917 — (IV)

Place	Date July	Hour	Summary of Events and Information	Remarks and references to Appendices
DESSART WOOD	25th		Coy. working on trench through Railway at R.8.c.99. C.T. through road at R.13.b. Sheltering C.T. R.14.b.9.3. Filters for B.H.Q. at R.13.d. 9/3. Tactical wire at R.19.a.6.5. 2nd duty, laying trench boards R.9.a. Work on woods R.36. r. R.25. R.30.3. No.99616. Sapper SMITH.A.E. wounded at R.14.2.6.5 by rifle fire and died after admission to Aid Pozn. 4 O.R. No 216129 Sapper FITCH.G. No.120758 Sapper DOYLE.M. No 109312 Sapper BELTON.C.E. No.103071 Purves TAYLOR.A joined Company as reinforcements.	A/
	26th		— At work as above. 1 Lieut. A.W. WARD-WALKER 19th R.W.F. to attached to Coy. for duty with 119th Inf. Bde. boho by.	A/
	27th		1 — At work as above — and at Theatre FINS. V.12.B.7.1.	A/
	28th		— At work as above.— and at FARM & AEROPLANE Ravine iron shelters. Effectives strength 7 Officers 211 O.R. Attached 4 officers 186 O.R.	A/
	29th		Coy at work on shelters in Support line R.14.b. shelters in FARM RAVINE and AEROPLANE RAVINE, trailing TYRE DUMP Tactical wiring at R.26 & Roof to Theatre at FINS. Attached Coy. trailing Support line R.7a. on Road R.36 R.25 and R.19.a.	A/
DANCY RAVINE	30th		Coy at work as above. Headquarters moved from DESSART WOOD to DANCY RAVINE Q.34.C.4.8.	A/
	31st		Coy at work on trench through Railway at R.8.c.7.6. Sapping C.T. VILLERS R.13.b.7.5. Bn. H.Q. shelters R.13.d.7.9. Draining TYRE DUMP. Erecting "NISSEN" hut at new Camp W.2.C. Wiring at R.20.a.5.9. Divisional Theatre FINS V.12.B.7.1. Dismantling & clearing DESSART WOOD billets.	A/

231st FIELD COMPANY R.E.
31 JUL. 1917

O.C. COMMANDING
231st FIELD COY. ROYAL ENGINEERS

Confidential

Vol 15

War Diary

of

231st Field Company
R E

From 1st August 1917
To 31st August 1917

WAR DIARY
INTELLIGENCE SUMMARY
(Erase heading not required.)

Army Form C. 2118

AUGUST (1)

Instructions regarding War Diaries and Intelligence Summaries are contained in F.S. Regs., Part II. and the Staff Manual respectively. Title Pages will be prepared in manuscript.

Place	Date August	Hour	Summary of Events and Information	Remarks and references to Appendices
DANCIM RAVINE.			Map referred to throughout 57c. S.E. 1/20000	
	1st		Company at work on C.T. through road to join DICK AVENUE at R.13.B. Shitholing forward line at R.14.B.8.5. Shelters in FARM RAVINE and AEROPLANE RAVINE, Erecting NISSEN HUTS at W.1.a. Wiring reserve line at R.14.a.6.5, Div. Theatre FINS V.12.b.7.3.	AP
	2nd		Coy. at work as above. Transport lines move to W.7.B.6.8.	AP
	3rd		Coy. at work as above. Take over new sector (BEAUCAMP sector)	AP
	4th		Company at work draining LEICESTER AVENUE Q.12.a.3.c. Work on infantry camps at b.2.c. Divisional Theatre V.12.b.7.1. Wiring Reserve Line R.13.b.9.2. OR Inf. Berning and deepening C.T. at R.7.d.	AP
			Effective strength. 7 Officers 211. O.R. Attached 4 Officers 180. O.R.	
	5th		Coy. at work as above.	
	6th		Shelters for Brigade H.Q. R.29.a. Improving ASHBY ALLEY R.7.d., Improving & draining LEICESTER AVENUE R.12.c.2.9. Erecting Winter Camp W.2.c. repairing road to BEAUCAMP W.17.a.9.10. FINS THEATRE V.12.b.7.1. Attached Inf. Berning & deepening C.T. R.7.d. Attached inf. move to new billets GOUZEAUCOURT - TRESCAULT Road Q.30.b.1.9.	AP
	7th		Coy. at work as above. No. 3 & 4 Sections move to advanced billets b.17.2. Sections move to DANCIM RAVINE. Attached Inf. Improving FINS road b.4. completing DART AVENUE R.13.b. Improving new billets Q.30.b.1.9. To billets for his sections.	AP
	8th		No 1 Section move to Def. Bell camp at W.2.c. Erecting Inf. Camp W.2.c. Having Camouflage to 4.b.2.8. Road repairing & laying trench boards R.29.b.0.5. Berning & Trenchboarding ASHBY AVENUE R.7.d.2.9. Deepening & electing LEICESTER AVENUE Q.12.c.1.8.	AP

WAR DIARY
or
INTELLIGENCE SUMMARY
(Erase heading not required.)

Army Form C. 2118

— AUGUST —
(11.)

Place	Date August	Hour	Summary of Events and Information	Remarks and references to Appendices
DANCING RAVINE.	9th		Coy at work as above. Attached Inf. wiring at R.8.C.	JH
	10th		At work as above.	JH
	11th		At work as above. One O.R. joined Company as reinforcement.	JH
	12th		Effective strength 7 Officers 212 O.R. Attached 3 Officers 171. O.R. Coy at work. Erecting winter camp to 2.C., resting FINS Theatre, Coy HQ ASHBY AVENUE R.7.a.3.8. Clearing trees in BEAUCAMP Q.12.a.0.2. Exploiting well Q.12.a.1.7. Attached Inf. wiring front line + carrying material R.8.C 7.8.	JH
	13th		Coy at work as above.	JH
	14th		Coy at work. Erecting winter camp to 2.C., resting FINS Theatre, Brigade bomb store Q.23.b.9.1, laying trench boards to Brigade HQ. LINCOLN AVENUE Q.17.d.7.8, Sinestepping and draining ASHBY ALLEY R.7.b+d. Draining LEICESTER AVENUE Q.12.c. Clearing trees from road Q.12.a.0.2, Exploiting well Q.12.a.1.3. Attached Inf. wiring front line R.8.C. 7.8.	JH
	15th 16th 17th 18th		Coy at Work as above. Effective strength 7 Officers 212 O.R.	JH
	19th 20th		Coy at work as above. Attached 3 Officers 170. O.R. One O.R. joined Company as reinforcement.	JH

WAR DIARY
INTELLIGENCE SUMMARY

(Erase heading not required.)

Army Form C. 2118

— AUGUST —
(III.)

Place	Date AUGUST	Hour	Summary of Events and Information	Remarks and references to Appendices
DANCIN RAVINE	21st		Coy. at work as above. No. 1 & 2. Sections moved to advanced billets at Q.30.b.1.9. No.3 Section moved to Infantry Camp at Q.2.c. No.4. Section to DANCIN RAVINE Q.34.c.4.8. Attached Inf. One O.R wounded.	A/1
	22nd		Coy at work on shelters intermediate line Q.18.c. Training LINCOLN AVENUE and DART AVENUE. R.7.c.4.3., Well at Q.12.d.2.2., Erecting Infantry Camp at W.2.c., FINS THEATRE. Duckboarding Q.24.b.0.4. Attached Inf. wiring at R.8.c.4.7. 3. O.R. joined Coy as reinforcements.	A/1
	23rd 24th 25th		Company at work as above	A/1
	26th		Effective strength 7 Officers 215 O.R. Attached 3 Officers 173 O.R. Coy. at work on shelters BEAUCAMP ROAD R.13.a and INTERMEDIATE LINE Q.18.c. Well at Q.12.d.2.2., Winter Camp at W.2.c. FINS Theatre V.12.b.1.7 Bomb Store at Q.24.c.0.3. Attached wiring at R.8.c.18.	A/1
	27th		Coy. at work as above. Attached Inf. on roads at Q.17, 23, 24, 30, 2. O.R. wounded.	A/1
	28th 29th 30th		Coy. at work as above.	A/1
	31st		Coy at work as above, and erecting camouflage at W.4.5. Attached Inf. wiring at Q.7.a.5.5 and on Roads at Q.23, 24, 30. Two O.R. joined Company as reinforcements	A/1

Major R.E.

Vol 16

Confidential

War Diary

of

231st (Field) Company R.E.

September 1917.

Volume No 16

WAR DIARY or INTELLIGENCE SUMMARY

Army Form C. 2118

SEPTEMBER 1917

(1)

Map referred to throughout 57⁵ S.E. ⅟₂₀,₀₀₀.

Place	Date Sept.	Hour	Summary of Events and Information	Remarks and references to Appendices
DANUM RAVINE	1ˢᵗ		Company at work on Shelters, BEAUCAMP ROAD R.13.a. & INTERMEDIATE LINE Q.18.c. Well at Q.12.d.2.2. WINTER CAMP W.2.c ~ W.3.c. DIVISIONAL THEATRE, FINS. V.12.b.1.7. Attached Infantry wiring at Q.7.a.5.5. ~ on Roads at Q.30. Q.24. ~ Q.23. Effective strength. 7 officers 216. O.R. Attached 3 officers. 166. O.R.	✓
	2ⁿᵈ		Coy. at work as above, and road work generally.	✓
	3ʳᵈ		do. ~ Shelters RHONDDA TRENCH. R.7.d.7.3 ~ ASHBY ALLEY POST R.7.b.7.3. Attached on Roads at Q.23. Q.24. Q.30. R.13 ~ R.19 wiring at R.7.9.	✓
	4ᵗʰ		No. 1 Section are relieved by No. 3 Section move to W.3.C. No. 2 Section move to Q.30.f.1.9. At work on Shelters BEAUCAMP ROAD ~ Intermediate Line. Well at Q.12.d.2.2. Winter Camps at W.2.c. W.3.c. Attached Infantry on Roads.	✓
	5ᵗʰ 6ᵗʰ 7ᵗʰ		Coy at work as above.	✓
	8ᵗʰ 9ᵗʰ		Coy at work as above and Gum Boot Store at R.13.b.2.5. No above. Effective strength. 7 officers 215. O.R. Attached 3 officers 177 O.R. Winter Camps at W.2.c. Well at Q.12.d.2.2. Gum Boot Store R.13.b.8.2 ~ R.13.a.2.7. Ashby Post. R.7.b.7.3. ~ Soup Kitchen at Q.12.b. Attached Infantry wiring	✓ ✓
	10ᵗʰ		Coy. at work as above	✓
	11ᵗʰ		do. ~ Camps for Coal officers at V.12.a.3.9.	
	12ᵗʰ 13ᵗʰ 14ᵗʰ 15ᵗʰ		Coy. at work as above. Effective strength 7 officers 216. O.R. Attached. 2 officers 183. O.R.	✓ ✓

WAR DIARY
or
INTELLIGENCE SUMMARY

Army Form C. 2118

SEPTEMBER (iii)

Place	Date SEPT	Hour	Summary of Events and Information	Remarks and references to Appendices
	16. 17. 18. 19.		Coy. at work as before	
	20.		Attached infantry firing from line. Coy. at work on Wurker Camps at W.3.C. Shelters at Q.17.6.1.8. Q.11.d.9.5. Well at Q.12.d.2.2. Widening Dick Avenue at R.14.6. Raining Surrey Ravine R.14.6.	BM
	21.		At work as above. Preparing for raid.	BM
	22.		Raid was carried out by 14 H.L.I. at enemy front line Sunken road in R.8.a. One Corporal + 8 O.R. R.E. accompanying the infantry, object being to destroy dug outs. Six return parties in enemy line. Infantry well in three waves, sappers going with each. Enemy two waves held no difficulty, sappers reached objective. One party of 3 bit 6 bangalore torpedoes, others shells (used as mobile charges). One party of entrances to 6 dug outs, object being to set dug out on fire one dug out turned out to be an ammunition dump & was exploded. Two other sapper blew return gap in enemy wire picked up two enemy prisoners & returned. Remaining Corporal & 3 sappers who went with 3rd wave were held up by enemy M.G. field no useful R.E. work, 2 becoming casualties. R.E. generally considered successful. Raid was preceded a few minutes by a demonstration of in which dummy figures (painted on flat) were used, worked by wire to Trench. They worked successfully, but shuffled of they drew much fire, they did undoubtedly contribute to clearing the enemy. However - E.F.ohn Staught Coy. 7 officers 216 o.R. attached 3.0.24d.o.R.	BM
	23.		Coy. at work on Shelters at R.13.F + Q.18.C. Gun Emplacement at 12.13. a.2.7 & R.13.B.2. and Q.11.d.2.2. Well at Q.11.d.9.5. Q.17.d. R.19.d. R.13.d. R.19.d. Q.17.d Q.23.C. New Latrines in Tresault Road Worker Camps W.2.C + W.3.C	BM
	24.		Coy. at work as above. Capt. F.W. Clark leaves Company to Command 209 X Field Coy. R.E.	BM

1875 W. W593/826 1,000,000 4/15 J.B.C. & A. A.D.S.S./Forms/C. 2118.

WAR DIARY or **INTELLIGENCE SUMMARY**

Army Form C. 2118

SEPTEMBER (iii)

Place	Date Sept.	Hour	Summary of Events and Information	Remarks and references to Appendices
	25.		Coy at work on shelters BEAUCAMP RD, INTERMEDIATE LINE, GUMBOOT STORE R.13.a.2.7	
	26.		WINTER CAMP W.2.C. WELL at Q.12.d.1.3. Attached working on Roads at R.19.d. R.13.c.	
	27.		Q.23.c. Q.17.d. wiring at R.7.c.	
	28.			
	29.		GUM BOOT STORE R.13.a.2.7. Shelters R.13.t. R.18.c. GUM BOOT STORE R.11.d. q.5.	
	30.		Erecting huts - Roads at W.2.c. - W.3.c. Well at Q.12.d.1.3. attached infantry	
			working on roads effective strength of Coy. 6 officers. 215- O.R. attached + off. 220 O.R.	
			Coy. at work as above.	

Army Form C. 2118

WAR DIARY
or
INTELLIGENCE SUMMARY
(Erase heading not required.)

OCTOBER 1917
(1)

Place	Date	Hour	Summary of Events and Information	Remarks and references to Appendices
DANUM RAVINE	1st		MAP REFERRED TO THROUGHOUT 57 S.E. 57DD0.	
			Coy. at work on Gum Boot Store R.13.b.8.2 & Q.11.d.9.5. Shelters at Q.11.b.2.8 Q.11.d.9.5. & Q.18.b.9.9. Winter Camps at W.3.C. & W.3.C. & Well at Q.12.d.1.3.	EW
	2.			EW
	3.		as above.	EW
	4.			EW
	5.		Company relieved by 88th Field Coy. R.E. move to W.3.C. Camp rare accumulated on Nissen Huts.	EW
	6.		Cleaning Camp. EFFECTIVE STRENGTH. 6 officers. 214 O.R. Marked. 32 O.R.	EW
	7.		Company repairing FINS - GOUZEAUCOURT ROAD.	EW
	8.		do.	EW
	9.		do.	EW
	10.		Company for duty. 2 Lieut W.H.NEWTON joined. Company at work as above. CAPT. F. DENTON Acting 2nd Dec. R.E. assumes Command of Company (temporarily) during absence of MAJOR JOHNSON on leave.	JD
	11.		At work as above & fixing Engine at Well at Q.36.b.6.3.	JD
	12.			JD
	13.		EFFECTIVE STRENGTH 7 officers. 213. O.R. Marked. 1 Officer 1.O.R.	JD
	14.		At work as above	
	15 & 16		Received order that CAPT.F.DENTON. Acting HO to Divisional R.E. appointed Second-in-Command (date 20th Sept 1917.)	JD
	17		Coy. at work as above.	JD

Army Form C. 2118

WAR DIARY
or
INTELLIGENCE SUMMARY

(Erase heading not required.)

OCTOBER 1917

Place	Date	Hour	Summary of Events and Information	Remarks and references to Appendices
	18th		Company move from W.2.C. proceed by Beauvoir to Peronne & remain the night.	
	19th		Transport move by road to Bapaume remain the night. Remainder of Company entrain at Peronne Flamicourt Station proceed to Beaumetz where they detrain and march to Berneville. EFFECTIVE STRENGTH 8 officers 212 O.R. At Berneville	
	20 to 27		Company training, wiring practice, overhauling lorries weapons. EFFECTIVE STRENGTH 8 officers 212 O.R.	
	28		Transport leave Berneville by road for Bapaume remain the night.	
	29		Bapaume proceed by road to Peronne. Remainder of Company leave Berneville entrain at Gouy-en-Artois for Peronne.	
	30		Company leave Peronne by road for Equancourt arrive 3.30 p.m	
	31		At Equancourt. Detached under III Corps for accommodation scheme at Fins.	

Newton Capt.
O.C 331 ? Coy R.E.

WAR DIARY
or
INTELLIGENCE SUMMARY
(Erase heading not required.)

Vol 231 Field Co RE
Vol 18

NOVEMBER 1917 (1.)

Place	Date	Hour	Summary of Events and Information	Remarks and references to Appendices
EQUANCOURT	1st to 3rd		Erecting shelter accomodation in Equancourt + Fins for nine Battalions. Effective strength 8 officers 212. O.R.	
	4th to 16th		Coy. at work as above	
	17th		Effective strength 8 officers 211. O.R.	
	18th		Coy. at work as above	
BEAULENCOURT	19th		Left EQUANCOURT 4.0 p.m. for BEAULENCOURT arrived 8.0 P.M.	
	20th		BEAULENCOURT 2.0 P.M. for BEAUMETZ-LES-CAMBRAI arrived 7.0 P.M.	
BEAUMETZ LES CAMBRAI	21		At BEAUMETZ-LES-CAMBRAI repairing bridge on the DEMICOURT-GRAINCOURT ROAD.	
	22			
	23		LEFT BEAUMETZ 2.0 A.M. for HAVRINCOURT arrived 9.30 a.m	
HAVRINCOURT	24		Effective strength 8 officers. 211. O.R.	
"	to		At HAVRINCOURT establishing nearing a line of defence in BOURLON WOOD.	
"	30		MAJOR F.H. JOHNSON V.C. reported killed in action 26th Nov.	

FHMDewter Cap IMC
OC 231 Fd Cy RE

Vol 19

CONFIDENTIAL.

WAR DIARY.

231st (Field) Company R.E.

DECEMBER 1917.

Vol 19

WAR DIARY
or
INTELLIGENCE SUMMARY
(Erase heading not required.)

Army Form C. 2118

Place	Date	Hour	Summary of Events and Information	Remarks and references to Appendices
HAVRINCOURT	1/2/17	—	At HAVRINCOURT - repairing roads.	
"	2nd			
"	3rd		Hon. ALLCROFT & Dvr RAWSON transferred to Mg. BASE DEPOT Company less Transport left HAVRINCOURT and marched to HAMELINCOURT where they arrived at 6.0 pm. The transport stayed the night at BEAULENCOURT.	
HAMELINCOURT - CROISILLES.				
"	5th		Arrival of transport at HAMELINCOURT - The company relieved the 157 Field Co R.E. in the CROISILLES SECTOR - 1 Off + 74 ORs attached to the company for work in the Nos. 2, 3 and 4 Sections moved to CROISILLES and were billeted at the CAVES - No. 1 Section	
"	6th		at HAMELINCOURT for work on Back Areas.	
"	7th		Sections forward employed on winning Intermediate line from U25a76 to U24b6.5 and 51 B.S.W and Strengthening wire in front of HUMBER SUPPORT U7d2.6 Work as above. Effective Strength - 7 Off 306 ORs attached wt. 1 Off 74 ORs	
"	8th			
"	9th		Winning Intermediate line - clearing + repairing trenches. No. 1 Section employed	
"	10th		on erecting camp for D.H.Q. at GOMIECOURT - 1 O.R. to hospital	
"	15		MAJOR J.E. NILLA, M.C. R.E. took over command of the Company from CAPTN DENTON R.E.	Rwj
"	15th		Effective Strength 7 officers 306 ORs attached 1 Off and 62 ORs	Rwj
"	16th		At work as above	
"	17th		Reclaiming TUNNEL TRENCH at U7d7.4 - Winning Burg Support at U7a work at Div. H.Q. GOMIECOURT	Rwj
"	18th		As above - work on Baths MOYENNEVILLE commenced	Rwj

WAR DIARY or INTELLIGENCE SUMMARY

Army Form C. 2118

(Erase heading not required.)

Place	Date	Hour	Summary of Events and Information	Remarks and references to Appendices
HAMELINCOURT & CROISILLES	19th		Work in reclaiming Tunnel Trench, wiring Schevardeli and Supports	R.S.
"	20th		Sunk CROISILLES SECTOR.	R.S.
"	21st		1 O.R. bone in shrapnel. HQ 40' Dinan	R.S.
"	22nd		Concentration on wiring of front line Support and Schevardeli	R.S.
"	23rd		Notification in London Gazette approved by mention of C.S.M. STEAD - mention in Despatch - CPL. WALKER R.A. awarded military medal for gallantry at BOURLON WOOD on NOV. 30.	R.S.
"	24th		Ceremonial Parade (2.w.) W. Corps Commander in presentation of above to recipients. 1 OFF. and 6 O.Rs. represented this company Effective Strength 8 OFF. 204 O.Rs. attached. 10 FF. 540 O.Rs. warning order received of impending move - side slipping southwards - 1 O.R. evacuated sick - Church Parade for Section in rear - half day work for submissions	R.S.
"	25th		Proceed in the morning. 1 O.R. evacuated to 20 CCS. Work in the BULLECOURT SECTOR taken over from 539 FIELD Co. R.E. Forward 1 Section at MORY.	R.S.
"	26th		Billets at ECOUST - headquarters and transport and 1 Section No. 3 Section relieved No. 1 Section.	R.S.
MORY & ECOUST	27th		Company HQ moved from HAMELINCOURT to MORY. Forward schemes of Completed. We have from CROISILLES to ECOUST by G.O. in Bullecourt HAMELINCOURT hand over to 503 field Co. RE. 34th Div.	R.S.
"	28th		Work on cleaning and nenewing Church - 2 O.Rs. reinforcements from Bose	R.S.
"	29th		Work in above. Effective Strength - Officers 30.6.08 attached infantry - 1 Officer 55 O.Rs.	R.S.

WAR DIARY
or
INTELLIGENCE SUMMARY
(Erase heading not required.)

Army Form C. 2118

Place	Date	Hour	Summary of Events and Information	Remarks and references to Appendices
MORY & ECOUST	29.12.17		Work on machine gun trenches.	961, 957, 967
"	30.		do	
"	31.		do — 1 O.R. joined company from Base.	

J. Wells, Major R.E.
O.C. 231 Field Co R.E.

Vol 20

Confidential.

War Diary

231st (Field) Company R.E.

January 1918.

Vol 20

WAR DIARY
or
INTELLIGENCE SUMMARY

Army Form C. 2118

JANUARY

Place	Date	Hour	Summary of Events and Information	Remarks and references to Appendices
MORY -ECOUST	1st		WORK Nos 1, 2 and 3 Sections at Forward Posts ECOUST - employed on general trench maintenance. No. 4 Section at MORY - Back Area work - reference to Camps - erection of new Stabling &c	
"	2nd		Work as above. 1 OR evacuated to clearing station - 7 ORs proceeded to U.K. on leave	
"	3rd		Work as above. 1 OR on leave returned from leave	
"	4th		Work as above - Heavy Shelling on our front line sector of Hindenburg complete block established as a result at junction of TANK AVENUE and front line - Infantry working parties under R.E. Supervision employed in clearing the Hindenburg front line	
"	5th		Work as above - Heavy Shelling of front line Hindenburg front line preceded an attack on our trenches at 6.35 am. The enemy came over in force and established a footing in our trenches at the junction of TANK AVENUE and the front line from which he was ejected by bombing operations but he succeeded in maintaining his hold of the sap head at U.30.c.2.4 having been ejected - 7 ORs on leave returned 6.30 p.m. when he was reported as Attached 103 OR 203 OR BQFF Station 9 hindered in attending of the front line above - our Captain very severely of the front wounded - parties were out clearing the whole	
"	6th		day. Work as above. Sub-Section Relief - Nos 1, 3, and 4 at ECOUST in work in the forward area No 2 Section at MORY in work in back areas Lt. KNIGHT - 7 ORs proceeded on leave to U.K.	
"	7th		Lt. NEWTON relieved Lt. KNIGHT - 7 OR's proceeded from ECOUST to DYSART CAMP in Cognecian 120. Rode Works Company were with a diminished order discontinuing the practice of having Works Companies	

WAR DIARY
INTELLIGENCE SUMMARY

Army Form C. 2118

Place	Date	Hour	Summary of Events and Information	Remarks and references to Appendices
MORY ECOUST	7th JANUARY		Took Companies affiliated to Field Companies and reflecting the Early by a Platoon from each Battalion of the 121st Bde. to whom the 231st Field Company is affiliated. Half of this party of Su O.Rs. only supplied today the arrival of the remainder being postponed on account of tactical considerations. No. 4 Section Relieved No. 2 Section in the line.	51
"	8"		Work 3 Sections forward and 1 section back as before. At 6.35 a.m. the enemy made another attack on our right section, using flammenwerfer detachments in the use of gas shells to attain his objective. He succeeded in taking our front line & trenches in our line down. TANK SUPPORT & the front line by the LONDON SUPPORT but he were finally ejected with the loss of 18 prisoners. In the evening the block made was filled with wire under sniper supervision.	907
"	9"		Work as above. One Trench from 30" W. of FOX TROT to LONDON SUPPORT in a southerly direction to TANK AVENUE taped out and dug by Pioneers (12" Yorks) party.	907
"	10"		Work as above. 7 O.Rs. proceeded on Leave. 4 O.Rs. returned from Leave. 1 O.R. joined Company as reinforcement. 20 O.Rs. attached to Company from Div. Base unit. Coy.	805
"	11"		Work as above. 30 O.Rs. attached to Company completes strength of works Company to 10 OFF. and 80 ORs. Lt. WILBURN Rt. returned to atrs. - 1 O.R. to Base. Lt. WILBURN RE. returned from Leave.	807
"	12"		5 O.Rs. returned from Leave. "V" Corps School. Company strength reduced to No. 6 Stationary Hospital. Company strength 9 Officers 707 OR. attached 1 Off., 69 ORs.	807

WAR DIARY
or
INTELLIGENCE SUMMARY
(Erase heading not required.)

Army Form C. 2118

Place	Date	Hour	Summary of Events and Information	Remarks and references to Appendices
MORY. ECOUST.	13th		3 Sections at ECOUST working on Trench maintenance – one section also HQ at MORY on work in Back areas.	
"	14th		Section Reinf. No.2 Section returns. No.3 Section forward – work carried on usual without a stop. Lt BALL RE and Corpl WIBBERLEY proceeded to Yth Corps School of Instruction.	
"	15th		Work on Tracks to past Fine Concentrates on, as the whole system of tracks in this Sector collapses owing to the rapid thaw that set in.	
			9. O.Rs returns from leave.	
"	16th		Work on Tracks (Ducktracks) – Lt POSTLETHWAITE and 1 O.R. proceeded on leave. – Lt WILBURN returns from Hospital.	
"	17th		Work on Tracks. H.Q.R.s returns from leave.	
"	18th		Work on Tracks. – Capt. F. DENTON RE proceeds to ALBERT to report for duty to C.E. Third Army (Authority – Third Army A/Allocaur of 13.11.18)	
"	19th		Work on Tracks abonit 197 O.Rs proceeds on leave. Company Strength 7 Officers – 3 O.Rs returns from leave.	
"	20th		Work on Tracks. – 4 O.Rs returns from leave. – Tracks complete.	
"	21st		Section Refit – Section 2.3+4 moving Nº1 to Back Area.	
"	22		Concentration – Cleaning Gts of salvage and attached Infantry in area.	
			RAILWAY RESERVE – 7 O.R, on leave.	

Army Form C. 2118

WAR DIARY
or
INTELLIGENCE SUMMARY
(Erase heading not required.)

Instructions regarding War Diaries and Intelligence Summaries are contained in F. S. Regs., Part II. and the Staff Manual respectively. Title Pages will be prepared in manuscript.

Place	Date	Hour	Summary of Events and Information	Remarks and references to Appendices
Mory-Ecoust.	23rd		Sections 2, 3 and 4 for work in Forward Areas. Employed in clearing and renewing wire. "A" Para... RAILWAY RES. TRENCH from BULLECOURT AV. to TANK AV. Section 1 employed in Back Area work.	QQY.
"	24th		6 O.R.s returned from leave — 3 O.R.s reinforcements from Base. Work as above.	QQY.
"	25th		Work as above — 7 O.R.s proceeded on leave.	QQY.
"	26th		Work as above — 5 O.R.s returned from leave. Coy. Pays. Sr. 70th, 199 O.R.s attached 1 Lt. - 93 O.R.s MORY. Tanks by Summaries Ferry.	QQY.
"	27th		Work as above — 2 O.R.s returned from leave.	QQY.
"	28th		Squadrons. Section Relief. Sections 1, 2 and 3 on forward areas. Work as above — MORY (including TUNNELLERS CAMP occupied, part by this Unit) Invaded Back Areas. — 7 O.R.s proceeded on leave. by enemy night flying squadrons in some.	QQY.
"	29th		Work as above. Rewiring along RAILWAY RES. complete to Right Battalion 91st (Canter. (Brigade). Rewiring to be continued on to TANK AV.	QQY.
"	30th		Work as above. — Lt. NEWTOM R.E. proceeded on leave.	QQY.
"	31st		Work as above.	QQY.

Ellis
Major R.E.
O.C. 93rd Field Company
1. 2. 18.

CONFIDENTIAL

— WAR DIARY —

— 231ST FIELD COY. R.E —

— FEBRUARY 1918 —

Vol 21

WAR DIARY or INTELLIGENCE SUMMARY

Army Form C. 2118

FEBRUARY (1)

Place	Date	Hour	Summary of Events and Information	Remarks and references to Appendices
MORY ECOUST	1.2.18		Work - 3 Sections forward (Nos 1,2 & 3) Reserve and General maintenance work in chains & resetting Railway track and work. Accidental injury to Sapper JONES No. 164751 of this company caused by the discharge of a revolver found in the trench by Private ROBERTS. 2212719 the Do's Middlesex Regt. Papers forwarded to Brigade for necessary action. Lt. POSTLETHWAITE returns from leave.	[sig]
"	2		Work as above - 50 O.Rs. returns from leave. Strength of Company	[sig]
"	3		7 Officers 198 O.Rs. attaches 15 Officers 109 O.Rs. Work as usual. Fox TROT Competition.	[sig]
"	3.		Work as above - 3 O.Rs. proceed on leave.	[sig]
"	4		Work as above. Intersection refief. Sections 1, 3 & 4 forward. 2 at Back area work	[sig]
"	5		Work as above - 5 O.Rs. returns from leave.	[sig]
"	6		Work as above - 5 O.Rs. returns from leave. 4 O.R. proceeded on leave to U.K.	[sig]
"	7		Work as above. MAJOR J.E. VILLA proceeded to R.E. School of Instruction G.H.Q	[sig]

War Diary or Intelligence Summary

Army Form C. 2118

FEBRUARY (2)

Place	Date	Hour	Summary of Events and Information	Remarks and references to Appendices
MORY-ECOUST.	8/2/18		Work as abnor. 1 N.C.O. to Third Army School of Instruction. 6 O.R. returned from Leave. 1 O.R. to H. 1 O.R. to C.R.E. H.Q.	EPD
	9.		Work. Nos 1, 3 Sections. Nos 1, 3 R. Friend, employed in clearing and re-setting Railway Reserve, Foxtrot Trench & London Reserve, also General Maintenance in the Line. 1 O.R. returned from Leave. 1 O.R. to H. 1 O.R. returned from No 7 R.E. Park. 1 O.R. evacuated to No 45 C.C.S.	EPD
	10.		Work as abnor. 4 O.R. returned from Leave.	EPD
	11.		Work as abnor. 2 O.R. to H. 3 O.R. accidentally wounded on Defence Scheme C.15.	EPD
	12.		Work. 3 O.R. returned from Leave. Defence Scheme C.15.	EPD
	13.		Work. 4 O.R. Proceeded on Leave. 1 O.R. Proceeded to No Dut Train on Temporary Duty. T.3.0.8.	EPD
	14.		Work as abnor. 1 O.R. returned from Leave. 1 O.R. to 40 Anti Gas Train on Duty. 7 O.R. returned from Leave. Re-inspection from Company.	EPD
	15.		Work as abnor. TB.6 6.3 to C.I.D. 1 O.R. evacuated. C.I.D. to T.30.B. 1 O.R. arrived 3 days Cdt. 1 O.R. evacuated.	EPD
	16.		Work. "Defence Scheme" C.I.D. to T.30.B. 4 O.R. Proceeded on Leave. 1 O.R. evacuated to No 49 C.C.S. No 6 R.E. Park. 1 O.R. to H. 1 O.R. evacuated to No 49 C.C.S. Lt. Newton returned from Leave.	EPD

WAR DIARY or INTELLIGENCE SUMMARY

Army Form C. 2118

FEBRUARY (3)

Place	Date	Hour	Summary of Events and Information	Remarks and references to Appendices
MORY - ECOUST - CROISILLES	19/2/18		Work as afor. C.I. to T.30.b. 1.O.R. returned to Bn from 40th Div. Train. 4 O.R. returned from leave.	E90
"	18.		Work as afor. 1.O.R. returned (overstaying leave) under escort. "Punishment Inspects 17 days Pay. R.W.	E90
	19.		Work as afor. 1.O.R. proceeds to 40th Div Signal Co. for test.	E90
	20.		Work as afor. 3 O.R. returned from leave. 1.O.R. returned from H.P.	E90
	21.		Work as afor. 1 Officer + 2 O.R. returned from VI Corps School of Infantry.	E90
	22.		Work as afor. 2 O.R. proceed on leave.	E90
	23.		Work as afor. 1.N.O.D. proceeded to VI Corps School of Infantry School. 2.O.R. James Cos" from Base. 3 O.R. returned from leave.	E90
	24.		Work as afor. 4 O.R. proceeding on leave.	E90
	25.		Work as afor. 1.O.R. returned from 40th Div R.S.K.O.	E90
	26.		Work as afor. 1.O.R. proceeded to 40th Bn R.E. H.Q. N.O.R. returned from leave. 1.O.R. to H.P.	E90
	27.		Preparing for move. 4 O.R. proceeds on leave. 1.O.R. proceeded Capt. R.T. Bayce	E90
	28.		Move from MORY to "BIENVILLERS - au - BOIS."	E90

1.3.18.

40th Divisional Engineers

WAR DIARY

231st FIELD COMPANY R.E.

MARCH 1 9 1 8

INTELLIGENCE SUMMARY

(Erase heading not required.)

Instructions regarding War Diaries and Intelligence Summaries are contained in F.S. Regs., Part II. and the Staff Manual respectively. Title Pages will be prepared in manuscript.

Place	Date	Hour	Summary of Events and Information	Remarks and references to Appendices
BEINVILLERS-AU-BOIS.	1st MARCH.		Division in G.H.Q Reserve and to hold itself in readiness to move at 24 Hours notice - Company Training - Affiliated to 120: Bde. MAJOR VILLA rejoined Company on completion of the Course at R.E school of Instruction for Senior Officers, BLENDECQUES. Command of the Company handed over by Capt. DOWSON RE to MAJOR VILLA	JBV.
"	2nd "	6.0 pm.	1. O.R. joined Company from Base as reinforcement - 5 O.R's returned from leave.	JBV.
"	3rd "	11:30 am	Company Training - 1 O.R. from Hospital - 4 O.R's proceeded on leave. Church Parade - One Hour's Drill and finished for the day - 2nd Corp'l. BLACKAMORE proceeded to vi Corps Gas School - 2 O.R's joined Corp? from Base as reinforcements. Pontoons & Trestle Equipment drawn from No 8 R.E. PARK ARRAS. - 1 O.R. returned from duty at No 8 R.E. PARK	JBV.
"	4th "	10.30 am	Company Training - Inspection of the Company by C.R.E. - 2. O.R.s proceeded to 137" Fd Amb? for Course in SANITARY DUTIES. - 4. O.R.s Returned from leave.	JBV.
"	5th "		Company Training - CAPT DOWSON R.E. proceeded on leave.	JBV.
"	6th "		Route March. 1 O.R to Hospital.	JBV.
"	7th "		Company Training - 3. O.R.s on a Lewis-Gun Course fo. Anti-Aircraft Defence. - 1 O.R. on leave. Company Training & Inspection of Division by the vi Corps Commander. The Company was	JBV.
"	8th "	3.0 pm.	Inspected with the 120. Bde. Group - 3 O.R's on leave.	JBV.
"	9.10 "		Company Training - Warning Order for Move received. 3. O.R. proceeded on Transfer to Forway - Base Depot SAVY. - 3. O.R.s on Leave. - 3. O.R.s	JBV.
HAMELINCOURT 10 " - BOISLEUX - (ARMAGH CAMP).		6.0 pm	joined Company reinforcements from Base (on 12th). Company moved from BEINVILLERS to ARMAGH CAMP. BEINVILLERS—BOISLEUX AU MONT R.D.	JBV.

1875   Wt. W593/826   1,000,000   4/15   J.B.C. & A.   A.D.S.S./Forms/C. 2118.

INTELLIGENCE SUMMARY

(Erase heading not required.)

Instructions regarding War Diaries and Intelligence Summaries are contained in F.S. Regs., Part II. and the Staff Manual respectively. Title Pages will be prepared in manuscript.

Place	Date	Hour	Summary of Events and Information	Remarks and references to Appendices
ARMAGH CAMP (BOISLEUX-HAMELINCOURT ROAD)	11"	6.30 pm	Company arrived Armagh Camp. 11.0 pm. Details (13 ORs) Surplus 1st echelon Bridging Equipment left in charge of Lt Newton at BEINVILLERS.	JBC
"	12"		Company Standing by - Training Programme Continued.	JBC
"	13"		do do do. 4 ORs from leave.	JBC
"	14"		do do do. 1 OR. from leave - 1 O.R. to H"s	JBC
"	15"		Corps Cookery School.	JBC
"	16"		do do do	JBC
"	17"		do do do. - 3. ORs proceeded on leave	JBC
"	18"		do do do returned from leave	JBC
"	19"		do do 4 ORs returned - details of work in the line received	JBC
"	20"		Orders for Relief of 3rd Brigade on the 21st. Rt. Section otherwise Commenced - Bombardment began 5.0 am - Enemy German otherwise Commenced. orders to Stand To. - 7.0 pm orders received to move to the Army line opposite HAMELINCOURT. At 9.0 pm Bridges were posted. Defence opposite this company to police the roads in the vicinity & out-	JBC
21st MIDDLESEX SPRAWLEY MEAULTE ROAD 20th MIDDLESEX	21"		ST. LEGER. Company remaining the Army Line all day with the Seg. 2nd Army Line on their left. the Div and the Pioneer battalion from the 30". or Middlesex being in our Right. The transport ordered to move	JBC

INTELLIGENCE SUMMARY

Instructions regarding War Diaries and Intelligence Summaries are contained in F.S. Regs., Part II. and the Staff Manual respectively. Title Pages will be prepared in manuscript.

Place	Date	Hour	Summary of Events and Information	Remarks and references to Appendices
IN TRENCHES opposite HAMELINCOURT	22nd		From ARMAGH CAMP, HAMELINCOURT to AYETTE. 1 O.R. from details Left behind with supplies Pit. killed by an aeroplane bomb at BEINVILLERS. 2 O.Rs returned from leave.	App.1
TRANSPORT at AYETTE				
IN TRENCHES	23rd	4.30 am	Captain returns in the army line. Defence Scheme Operation Orders issued by the Shah awards 31st Division and orders to relieve the 6th Rifle	App.1
IN FRONT OF BEHAGINIES TRANSPORT at BUCQUOY		10 am	Defence in rear of BEHAGINIES. Order of Battle P.O.Cage Move to BEHAGINIES completed. The line consolidated – K.29.d – 229. 22.4 and Runners with us on the Right of the 23.1st Sea. Co' Company Transport of Lewis Guns from AYETTE to a camp in the West Side of the BUCQUOY – HANNESCAMPS Road – Capt. DAWSON and D.O.Rs returns from moonlight line and occupied in dug-in Company reliefs from moonlight.	App.90 App.90
"		7.0 pm	A line of Posts between GOMIECOURT and BEHAGNIES Consolidation of line. Patrolling and connecting up. Settles in at work in Pain – Mann Valley behind BEHAGINIES a machine gun opens fire on three from the direction of SAPIGNIES. This continues with a Scouse bombardment on the right and Left. The BEHAGINIES sector but an outbreak for the time being	
"	24	10.0 pm	A few posts in course of consolidation were manned. It was reported that the enemy had broken thro' at SAPIGNIES and a line was ERVILLERS a cross. The reserve proves to was a live wire.	App.1

INTELLIGENCE SUMMARY

(Erase heading not required.)

Instructions regarding War Diaries and Intelligence Summaries are contained in F.S. Regs., Part II. and the Staff Manual respectively. Title Pages will be prepared in manuscript.

Place	Date	Hour	Summary of Events and Information	Remarks and references to Appendices
	25th	1.0 a.m	Opposite GOMIECOURT and a report made to the CRE to that effect. The night passed was in the direction of GOMIECOURT. So the work was in progress & it was decided by 1.0 a.m reported to the C.R.E in person & it was decided that it was futile to now and work should be resumed; & this was done and completed by 5.0 a.m. Company orders to a camp in rear of	
		6.30 a	GOMIECOURT. This move was completed by 6.30 a.m. from here the Company moved to COURCELLES. Complete by R.R. mobilisation	
		12.30	So as to be available for defence of Railway Cutting if necessary.	
		1.0 pm	Boulogne arrived @ COURCELLES and to the huts in which Class 1 had been resting. Avenues of defence being taken up none COURCELLES.	
		3.0 pm	Orders received from CRE to concentrate at transport but then we found that they had	907
MONCHY AU BOIS		7.0 pm	in Busquoy but when we got there we found the Camp before. arrived in the open. Orders received to leave the Camp before	
	26.3.18.	8.0 am	I.D.R. wounded	
BEINVILLERS AU BOIS	26th	6.0 am	Company moved with transport to BEINVILLERS. Wire received that the enemy were advancing from HEBUTERNE	
		8.0 pm	in tanks on to the night Kent Orders received to proceed	907

INTELLIGENCE SUMMARY

(Erase heading not required.)

Instructions regarding War Diaries and Intelligence Summaries are contained in F.S. Regs., Part II. and the Staff Manual respectively. Title Pages will be prepared in manuscript.

Place	Date	Hour	Summary of Events and Information	Remarks and references to Appendices
BEINVILLERS	26"		BEINVILLERS - HANNESCAMPS Road and BEINVILLERS - FONQUEVILLERS Road in descention - a part of the company in defence of HELENTOIR. Report by Captain of HELENTOIR - a false alarm - men returned to billets at BEINVILLERS.	907
		8.0 pm		907
		10.0 pm	Orders received to leave BEINVILLERS by 7.0 am on 27.3.18	907
GOUY EN ARTOIS	27"	4.30 am	Company moved to GOUY-EN-ARTOIS and rested there.	907
SOMBRIN		4.0 pm	Company moved to SOMBRIN - T.O.R. immediately seeing aeroplane	907
		7.0 pm	Arrived at SOMBRIN.	
"	28"		Company resting - materials of kit and equipment - warm. Orders received of a move at 7.30 am 29.3.18	907
ROCOURT	29"	9.30 am	March with 120 Bde Group to ROCOURT. - Arrived ROCOURT 4.30 p.m.	907
SAILLY SUR LYS - FLEURBAIX	30"	11.00 am	March to DIEVAL and embussed - Arrived NERF BERQUIN 4.30 pm from which place the company marched to temporary billets between SAILLY and FLEURBAIX	907
BAC ST MAUR (SAILLY)	31st	12.0 Noon	Took over details of work etc from 502 (WESSEX) Field Co 57th Division - Moved into billets occupied by 502 Field Coy at BAC ST MAUR	907

J. Circle. Major R.E.
O.C. 231 Field Co.
31/3/18.

40th Divisional Engineers

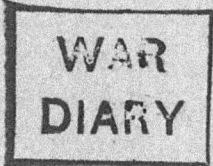

231st FIELD COMPANY R. E.

APRIL 1918

Vol 22.

CONFIDENTIAL

WAR DIARY

231st (Field) Company R.E.

April 1918.

Army Form C. 2118

WAR DIARY
or
INTELLIGENCE SUMMARY
(Erase heading not required.)

Instructions regarding War Diaries and Intelligence Summaries are contained in F. S. Regs., Part II. and the Staff Manual respectively. Title Pages will be prepared in manuscript.

Place	Date	Hour	Summary of Events and Information	Remarks and references to Appendices
BAC ST MAUR (FLEURBAIX SECTOR)	APL 1st		Reconnaissance of new Area (FLEURBAIX SECTOR) taken over from 51st Divisional R.E. (502 WESSEX Field Company).	637
	" 2nd		Work on Battle Zone and Emergency Bridges	637
	" 3rd		do. do. do. 6 O.Rs from leave.	637
	" 4th		do. do. do. 1 O.R. do Hospital.	637
	" 5th		do. do. do.	637
	" 6th		do. do. do. Wiring River LAIES commenced	637
	" 6th		1 O.R. wounded. SERGT BODDY joined Company from Base. Strength of Company, 7 Officers, 198 O.Rs.	637
	" 7th		Work on wiring River LAIES, Battle Zone and Emergency Bridges.	637
	" 8th		1 O.R. from leave.	637
	" 9th		Work on wiring River LAIES.	637
BAC ST MAUR	" 9th	4.30 a.m	Enemy offensive commenced. Bridge Mobilisation ordered 5.0 a.m. Bridges mobilised 8.45 a.m. Company Billet at BAC ST MAUR evacuated owing to heavy shelling. H.Q. and 2 & 3 Sections on N. side of River LYS. 1 Section Light and Pontoon Bridges destroyed between 2.0 p.m and 5.0 p.m and a line of defence taken up on the N. bank of the River LYS.	637
CUL DE SAC FARM		4.0 pm	Company Headquarters changed to near CUL DE SAC FARM (G14.b.1.5) so as to take up a position behind the Line of defence. Demolition of Ponts PONT LEVIS, ESTAIRES attempted but proved a failure owing to faulty fuses. LT. BALL M.C. wounded. 1 O.R. KILLED 19. OR's wounded	637
RUE PRUVOST (near NEUF BERQUIN)	" 10th	5.0 a.m 1.0 pm	Company Headquarters changed to vicinity of RUE PRUVOST near NEUF BERQUIN by order of C.R.E. Company Transport also there.	637

1875 Wt. W593/826 1,000,000 4/15 J.B.C. & A. A.D.S.S./Forms/C.2118.

WAR DIARY
or
INTELLIGENCE SUMMARY

Army Form C. 2118

Place	Date	Hour	Summary of Events and Information	Remarks and references to Appendices
RUE PRUVOST (near NEUF BERQUIN)	APRIL 10th	3·0 pm	Orders received for the Company to move into line again under orders of G.O.C. 119th Bde. for defence of LE VERRIER. A line of defence accordingly taken up astride the STEENWERCK – LE VERRIER Road. This was changed in an hours time	Rev7
LE VERRIER		4·30 pm	and the Company were ordered to move into the front line to fill a gap on the left	
STEENWERCK	" 11th		Lt. BALL M.C. reported Died of Wounds on the 9th. The left flank was the 88th Bde, 29th Division, the right flank details of the LOYAL NORTH LANCS who were under orders of the 150th Bde. The line taken up was from A.15. central through G.21.b.2.7. No order of battle being 2·29th Tellboo on the left, 2·4th Suffolks + 2·31st Suffolks owing to the flanks falling back, the line drifted back on to MAISON BLANCHE when the Divisional R.E. were relieved by 31st Division. 2. O.R.s KILLED + O.R.s wounded.	Rev7
STRAZEELE@ PRADELLES Road	"	6 pm	Company concentrated at Horse Lines on the STRAZEELE - PRADELLES Road. Orders received for a move next morning to HAZEBROUCK to vestrain when the Company had reformed.	Rev7
	" 12th	9·0 am	Company arrived at Horse Lines having rested at BAILLEUL. Orders for entrainment at HAZEBROUCK cancelled owing to situation and Company remained at above Headquarters. Transfer moved to HONDIGHEM. 9·0 am 20th, and 121st Bdes. Sappers ent all	
		5·0 pm	Company ordered to dig lines of defence for 120th 121st Brigades night at work	
	" 13th	2·0 p.m	Sappers employed on digging lines of defence for 120th 121st Brigades. Orders for concentration of R.E. at "Transport Lines" received at 2·0 p.m.	Rev7
		4·0 p.m	Company marched with Divisional R.E. and Pioneers to Transport Lines at HONDIGHEM.	

WAR DIARY or INTELLIGENCE SUMMARY

Army Form C. 2118

(Erase heading not required.)

Place	Date	Hour	Summary of Events and Information	Remarks and references to Appendices
MAISON BLANCHE	Apl. 13th		Arrived HONDIGHEM (Transport Train) at 6.0 p.m. had a meal & moved on to MAISON BLANCHE on the CASSEL-ARQUES Road where they arrived at 10.0 p.m. and stayed the night there.	907
CORMETTE	" 14th	10:30 am	Strength of Company 6 Officers, 155 O.R.s. Company moved with the Divisional R.E. and Pioneers in the 119th Brigade attacks to CORMETTE. Arrived at CORMETTE 5.30 p.m.	907
"	" 15th		Company rested. Refitting of Company commenced.	907
"	" 16th		Inspection of the Divisional R.E. by C.R.E. in Chateau grounds CORMETTE	907
"	" 17th		Company Training.	907
"	" 18th		Inspection of Divisional R.E. by G.O.C. 40th Division. Reinforcement of 12 O.R.s which arrived for the Company yesterday are posted to 224 Field Company which is being made up to strength so as to have one Field Company complete for emergencies.	907
"	" 19th		Company Training – Range Practices	907
"	" 20		Company Training – Range Practices. Effective Strength 6 officers 167 O.R.s.	907
ZUTOVE	" 21st	4:30 pm	Company moved independently to ZUTOVE	907
"	" 22		Reconnaissance made of HERZEELE – LE BREARDE line in front of ST SYLVESTRE-CAPPEL. Orders received to move to SYLVESTRE under instructions of C.R.E. 9th Corps Troops.	907
ST SYLVESTRE CAPPEL	" 23rd	8.0 am	Transport under CAPT DOWSON proceeded by road and dismounted personnel in Buses to ST SYLVESTRE-CAPPEL. Arrival 3.0 p.m. Billets in farm at P.24 central on the ST SYLVESTRE – STEENVOORDE Road.	907

WAR DIARY
or
INTELLIGENCE SUMMARY

(Erase heading not required.)

Instructions regarding War Diaries and Intelligence Summaries are contained in F.S. Regs., Part II. and the Staff Manual respectively. Title Pages will be prepared in manuscript.

Place	Date	Hour	Summary of Events and Information	Remarks and references to Appendices
ST SYLVESTRE CAPPEL	April 24		Work commenced on HERDZEELE-LA BREARDE LINE under C.R.E. VIII Corps Troops - Company working on Right Sector with 224th Field Coy under Lt. Col. Barney C.R.E. H.Q. PIPPERS in the Centre Sector. Right Sector taken over by C.R.E. 40th Division - Company at work in same sector.	W.
	25		Work on Army Line defences continued	W.
	26		Work on Army Line defences continued. Lt. Price +4 O.R.s from 4/5th Manchesters from 66th Division attached to the Company. Effectives strength of Company - 6 officers 167 OR's attached 1 officer 4 ORs	W.
	27		Work on Army Line defences continued. 833rd Labour Company arrived in billets to work in Army Line. Reporting for work to me now - took letter over from 218th Field Coy working on our right to LA BREARD	W.
	28		Order received from C.R.E. 40th Division for work to cease on the Right Sector as it had been handed over to 4th Division - 833rd Labour Company commenced work on the Right Sector but closed work on completion of works allotted	W.
CORNHUYSE (N. of Cassel)	29	2.0 p.m	Company moved to CORNHUYSE to recent work 224th Field Company in Centre Sector now called the Right Sector, there being only two Sectors - Company billeted in farms.	W.
	30		Work commenced on the new Right Sector - Company employed on running 2 sections on the support line + 2 sections on the main line of Resistance	W.

Villa Moynch
1/5/18. OC 231 Fd Coy.

1875 Wt. W593/826 1,000,000 4/15 J.B.C. & A. A.D.S.S./Forms/C. 2118.

Vol 24

Confidential

War Diary

231st (Field) Company R.E.

May 1918

Vol 23

Army Form C. 2118

WAR DIARY
or
INTELLIGENCE SUMMARY
(Erase heading not required.)

Instructions regarding War Diaries and Intelligence Summaries are contained in F. S. Regs., Part II. and the Staff Manual respectively. Title Pages will be prepared in manuscript.

Place	Date	Hour	Summary of Events and Information	Remarks and references to Appendices
CORNYHUSE	1.5.18		WORK ON WINIZEELE LINE. (No 4 Sector) Lieut Cruchard - 4 Sections wiring.	JES
"	2.5.18		Work as above - LT. KNIGHT R.E. (temporarily attached to 229th Field Co. R.E. for work on the left half of the WINIZEELE LINE.	JES
"	3.5.18		Work as above - 1 O.R. to hospital	JES
"	4.5.18		Work as above - Effective Strength: 7 Company - 6 Officers and 166 ORs	JES
"	5.5.18		Work as above - Information received (D.R.O. 1949 of 3/5/18) that 106803 SERGT BATES and 107096 2/Cpl. BENISTONE W.H. has been awarded Military Medals for gallantry and devotion to duty during Operations carried out by the Division between March 21st and March 26th 1918.	JES
"	6 "		Work as above - 1 O.R. to hospital.	JES
"	7 "		Work as above - 10.R. to hospital. Capt. DOWSON R.E. proceeded on special leave to United Kingdom. 2nd Lt. BURT R.E. arrived as reinforcement to 7th Company from Base. - 25 ORs reinforcement from Base posted to the Company.	JES
"	8 "		Work as above. -	JES
"	9 "		Work as above - 2/Lt. KNIGHT rejoined Company. - 1 O.R. to convals Company.	JES
"	10 "		Work as above - LT. WILBURN attached to 40" Division as S.O. R.E. to MAJOR GEN. KENYON.	JES

WAR DIARY
or
INTELLIGENCE SUMMARY
(Erase heading not required.)

Army Form C. 2118

Place	Date	Hour	Summary of Events and Information	Remarks and references to Appendices
CORNHUYSE	10th		Work on WINIZEELE LINE (N° 4 Sector) continued — 4 Sections Employed on lining — Effective Strength of Company — 7 Officers and 190 ORs — 10R joined Company as reinforcement from Base	—
"	12th		Work as above — 10.R. to Hospital	—
"	13th		Work as above — 1 OR evacuated	—
"	14th		Work as above — 10.R. evacuated	—
"	15th		Work as above —	—
"	16th		Work as above — 1 OR evacuated	—
"	17th		Work as above — 1 O.R. joins Company from Base — 2.O.Rs evacuated —	—
"	18th		Work as above. Effective Strength of Company — 7 Off. and 187 ORs. MAJOR J.E.VILLA proceeded on Special Leave to Chalôns Bougnon. + Lt. W. B. Postlethwaite took over Command. 1.O.R. Joined Company.	—
"	19th		Notification received that 22855 Sgt BUCKLEY T.H + N°107322 A/2/Cpl Kidson W had been awarded the Military Medal for Gallantry + Devotion to duty during operations between April 9th 1973th 1918. (D.R.O. 1970 d/18/5/18) Work as above — 1.O.R. evacuated	—

WAR DIARY
or
INTELLIGENCE SUMMARY

Army Form C. 2118

Place	Date	Hour	Summary of Events and Information	Remarks and references to Appendices
CORN HUYSE	20th		Work as above - in WINIZEELE LINE (N° 4 SECTOR).	nor.
	21st		Work as above.	nor.
	22nd		Work as above.	nor.
	23rd		Work as above.	nor.
	24th		Work as above.	nor.
	25th		Work as above - 2 SECTIONS (N°S 1 & 2) moved to THORLANDS DUMP P24a 5.2. to work under C.R.E. N° 1 SECTOR. WORK. Wiring Main line & Resistance.	nor.
	26th		Effective Strength of Company & Officers 184 O.R. - 2 O.R. rejoined Unit. Work as above - 11 O.R. rejoined Company from 224 FIELD C°.	nor.
	27th		Work as above - 1. O.R. Evacuated.	nor.
	28th		Work as above - 1. O.R. "	nor.
	29th		Work as above -	nor.
	30th		Work as above -	nor.
	31st		Work as above -	nor.

W. P. Postlethwaite L.R.E.
for O.C. 231st Fd C° R.E.

Vol 25

Confidential
War Diary
231st (Field) Company R.E.
         June 1918.

Volume 25

WAR DIARY
or
INTELLIGENCE SUMMARY

(Erase heading not required.)

Army Form C. 2118

Instructions regarding War Diaries and Intelligence Summaries are contained in F. S. Regs., Part II. and the Staff Manual respectively. Title Pages will be prepared in manuscript.

Place	Date	Hour	Summary of Events and Information	Remarks and references to Appendices
CORNHUYSE	1st June		Working WINIZEELE Line = Capt Browne returns from leave. Effective strength 7 officers and 187 O.Rs. Section under Cpl M¹ Smith and Italian under Cpl Murrell. Work as above.	905? 900?
"	2ⁿᵈ "		Work as above.	935
"	3ʳᵈ "		Work as above. Major J.E. Yule returned from leave.	934 (935)
"	4ᵗʰ "		Work as above. — 1. O.R. transferred to R.E. Base Depot — 1. O.R. to Hospital	937
"	5ᵗʰ "		Work as above	936
"	6ᵗʰ "		Work as above	937
"	7ᵗʰ "		Work as above — 1. O.R. proceeded on leave to U.K. — 1. O.R. from Hospital	937
"	8ᵗʰ "		Effective Strength 7 officers and 186 O.Rs	937
CAMP ON HONDEGHEM HAZEBROUCK (V15a 5.1).	9ᵗʰ "		9ᵗʰ Headquarters and 2 Sections from CORNHUYSE to camp on HONDEGHEM HAZEBROUCK Road for instruction from PARACHUTE Un Company WEST HAZEBROUCK (WEST HAZEBROUCK LINE) at this camp for work on WEST HAZEBROUCK LINE	937 935
"	10ᵗʰ		4 Sections on WIRING — WEST HAZEBROUCKE LINE	937
"	11ᵗʰ		Work as above — 1. O.R. evacuated	937
"	12ᵗʰ "		Work as above	935
"	13ᵗʰ "		Work as above	935
"	14ᵗʰ "		Work as above — 2 O.R. to Hospital. Effective Strength of Company 7 officers + 185 O.Rs	937
"	15ᵗʰ "		Work as above — 1 O.R. to Hospital. Warning order received to warm near HAZEBROUCK LINE in the event of hostile action on the 2ⁿᵈ Army front	937
"	16ᵗʰ "			939

1875 Wt. W593/826 1,000,000 4/15 J.B.C. & A. A.D.S.S./Forms/C.2118.

WAR DIARY
or
INTELLIGENCE SUMMARY
(Erase heading not required.)

Army Form C. 2118

Place	Date	Hour	Summary of Events and Information	Remarks and references to Appendices
CAMP ON HONDEGHEM - HAZEBROUCK ROAD (V.17.a.5.1)	17.5		A Section wiring WEST HAZEBROUCKE LINE. 1 O.R. injured. Company reinforcement work no alum.	9/07
"	18.5		1 O.R. to hospital and returned the same day from pains.	9/07
"	19.5		Company Rest day owing to shortage of mining materials — Box Repeater. Inspection and arms came out by all Ranks.	9/07
"	20.5		Work on mining WEST STRAZEEBROUCK LINE continued.	9/07
"	21.5		Work on mining WEST STRAZEEBROUCK LINE continued.	9/07
"	22.5		Work on mining continued. SAPPER HEMINGWAY J.C. awarded Meritorious Medal in Birthday Honours List. Strain in Rifle and Section Inspection.	(9)
"	23.5		1 O.R. evacuated to C.C.S. Company Rest Day. General Rifle and Kit Inspection - 1 O.R. to Base Depot - 1 O.R. evacuated to hospital.	83
"	24.5		Work on WEST HAZEBROUCK Line Mining & Cavaliers - 3 O.Rs. to hospital.	85
"	25.5		Work on WEST HAZEBROUCK line cont'd - 3 O.Rs. Joined Company as reinforcement from Base.	85
"	26.5		Work as usual.	85
"	27.5		Practice Concentration at V.19.c and V.20. for the event of enemy attack.	83
"	28.5		1 O.R. to hospital.	83
"	29.5		Work on Hazebrouck Line continued. 2/Lieut. Shingle 7 Mon. 18th Bn.	83
"	30.5		taking over of the Company by C/Lt 40th Division.	83

Ewell Major R.E.
O.C. 23rd Div. R.E.

CONFIDENTIAL.

War Diary

231st (Field) Company R.E.

July 1918

Volume 26

WAR DIARY
or
INTELLIGENCE SUMMARY

(Erase heading not required.)

Army Form C. 2118

JULY 1918

Instructions regarding War Diaries and Intelligence Summaries are contained in F.S. Regs., Part II. and the Staff Manual respectively. Title Pages will be prepared in manuscript.

Place	Date 1918	Hour	Summary of Events and Information	Remarks and references to Appendices
CAMP ON HONDEGHEM - HAZEBROUCK ROAD V.15.a.5.1.	1st July		4 Sections Wiring and improving System of Trenches, WEST HAZEBROUCK LINE	
	2nd "		Work as above. 1 O.R. to hospital. 2 O.R. evacuated.	
	3rd "		Work on WEST HAZEBROUCK LINE continued.	
	4th "		" " " " "	
	5th "		" " " " "	
	6th "		" " " " " 1 O.R. returned from Hospital	
	7th "		" " " " " 1 O.R. transferred to 206th FD.C.Y.R.E. Effectives Strength 7 Offrs. 180 O.R.	
	8th "		Company Rest day. Box respirator, Rifle kit inspection. 1st POSTLETHWAITE proceeded on Leave E.UK	
	9th "		Work on WEST HAZEBROUCK LINE continued.	
	10th "		" " " " " 1 O.R. rejoins company from Hospital. 1 O.R. evacuated.	
	11th "		" " " " "	
	12th "		" " " " " 8 O.R. joined Company from Base Depot.	
	13th "		" " " " "	
	14th "		" " " " " Effective Strength 7 Offrs. 188 O.R.	
	15th "		Company Rest day. Box respirator, Rifle Kit and Medelyabata [?] Stan chest. 1 O.R. joined Comp. from Base Depot.	
	16th "		Work on WEST HAZEBROUCK LINE continued. Major VILLA M.C.R.E. fits up temporary duties as A/CRE 20th Division	
	17th "		Capt DOWSON assumed Command of Company.	
	18th "		Work as above. 2nd Lt KNIGHT proceeded on Leave E.UK. Company Sports 5.0 PM 6.0 PM	
	19th "		" " " " " 5.0 PM 8.0 PM	
	20th "		" " " " " Inspection of Camp by Major General Sir J.F. PEYTON. K.C.B, K.C.V.O, D.S.O, G.O.C. 20th Division.	
	21st "		" " " " " 2 O.R. Proceed on Leave E.UK.	
	22nd "		" " " " " Effective Strength 7 Offrs. 169 O.R.	
	23rd "		Company Rest day. Box respirator, Rifle kit inspection. 40th Divl R.E. Sports.	
	24th "		Work on WEST HAZEBROUCK LINE continued. 1st POSTLETHWAITE returned from Leave 6 O.K. 1st WILBURN rejoined Comp from 40th Division	
	25th "		" " " " "	
	26th "		" " " " " 1 O.R. proceeded on Leave E.UK.	
	27th "		" " " " " A/D.Q.S/Harris/C. 2118. Company from Base Depot. Effective Strength 7 Offrs. 209 O.R.	

WAR DIARY
or
INTELLIGENCE SUMMARY

(Erase heading not required.)

Army Form C. 2118

Place	Date 1918	Hour	Summary of Events and Information	Remarks and references to Appendices
Camp on Hondeghem — Hazebrouck Road V.15 a 5.1	28th July		Company Rest day Box respirator Rifle and kit inspection	[sgd]
	29th "		Work on West Hazebrouck Line continued	[sgd]
	30th "		" " " " " "	[sgd]
	31st "		" " " " " "	[sgd]

E. Dodson Capt RE
O/C 105th Field Coy RE

31/7/18.

CONFIDENTIAL.

—WAR DIARY—
—231st (Field) Company, R.E.—

Vol 27

AUGUST, 1918

WAR DIARY
or
INTELLIGENCE SUMMARY

(Erase heading not required.)

Army Form C. 2118

Instructions regarding War Diaries and Intelligence Summaries are contained in F. S. Regs., Part II. and the Staff Manual respectively. Title Pages will be prepared in manuscript.

Place	Date 1918	Hour	Summary of Events and Information	Remarks and references to Appendices
CAMP in HONDEGHEM HAZEBROUCK Rd V.15.a.5.1	August 1st		4 Sections, Wiring and improving System of Trenches, WEST HAZEBROUCK LINE. Lt KNIGHT R.E. returned from Leave to U.K. 1 O.R. proceeded on Leave to U.K.	EWD
do	" 2nd		Work on WEST HAZEBROUCK LINE. Continued. 1 O.R. comands. 1 O.R. returned from Course at XV Corps. Lewis Gun School	EWD
do	" 3rd		Work as above. Effective Strength 7 Officers 199 O.R.	EWD
do	" 4th		Company Rest day. Bne respirator, Rifle and Kit inspection. 1 O.R. returned from Course at R.E. School of Instruction, ROUEN	EWD
do	" 5th		Work on WEST HAZEBROUCK LINE. Continued. 1 O.R. returned from Leave to U.K. 3 O.R. joined Company as reinforcements from Base.	EWD
do	" 6th		Work as above. Major HILL M.C., R.E. rejoined Company from 3/o to Base Engineer, 1 O.R. Remanded Leave to U.K. 1 O.R. proceeded to Course at R.E. School of Instruction, ROUEN, 1 O.R. joined Company as reinforcement from Base.	EWD
do	" 7th		Work on WEST HAZEBROUCK LINE Continued.— 10 Labour Companies	EWD
do	" 8th		Work as above. — Lt NEWTON proceeded to XV Corps Lewis Gun School at OUDEZEELE.	Rep
do	" 9th		Work as above. — 1 O.R. proceeded on Leave to U.K.	do
do	" 10th		Effective Strength 7 Officers 7 Officers 204 Other ranks - 1 O.R. transferred from the 64th Field Company R.E. — 10 O.R. returned from leave	do
do	" 11th		Company Rest day. — Rifle and Box Respirator inspection carried out. 10 O.R. proceeded on Leave to U.K. — 10 O.R. to Lewis Gun Course at Le TOUQUET.	do
do	" 12th		Work on Aircraft Hangers. Lieut continues. Lt WILBURN attached to Moorgreen R.S. for Duty as Assistant Adjutant.	Rep

1875 Wt. W593/826 1,000,000 4/15 J.B.C. & A. M.D.S.S./Forms/C.2118.

WAR DIARY or INTELLIGENCE SUMMARY

Army Form C. 2118

Place	Date	Hour	Summary of Events and Information	Remarks and references to Appendices
CAMP - HONDEGHEM - HAZEBROUCK Rd. (VIS or 5/1 Sheet 27)	Aug. 13th	—	Work on WEST HAZEBROUCK LINE continued – training to continue for the Company to carry on work on the EAST HAZEBROUCK LINE under C.R.E. XV Corps Troops on and from the 14th. But owing to the G.V. Field Company whom we are relieving not going out of the area till the 16th, work was not taken over.	
	14th		Work on West Hazebrouck Line temporarily stopped.	
	15th		Work on East Hazebrouck Line under C.R.E. 2nd Corps Troops commenced. 1. O.R. proceeds on leave to U.K.	
	16th		4. O.Rs. Joins Company from Base. 5 O.Rs. proceeds on L.G. course to 17th Bat. Worcester Reg: (Ko Doll Runners) Work on East Hazebrouck Line continued. Strength of the Company over to do. 1. O.R. returns from leave. Effective Strength of the Company handed over to do. 1. O.R. returns from leave.	
	17		Work on East Hazebrouck Line — 1 Officer 30 & ORs on leave UK.	
	18th		Hqrs A.T. Company – 1.O.R. on leave UK. Work on West Hazebrouck Line resumed – 1 OR proceeds on leave UK. 1 Officer Cadet arrived in R.A.F. – 1.	
	19th		Company Rest Day in lieu of the 17th owing to Divisional Horse Show. – 1.O.R. Joined Company from Base Repl.	
	20th		LT. NEWTON admitted to Army Gen. Hospital from XV Corps School suffering from injuries to the Knee.	

WAR DIARY
or
INTELLIGENCE SUMMARY

(Erase heading not required.)

Army Form C. 2118

Place	Date	Hour	Summary of Events and Information	Remarks and references to Appendices
CAMP HONDEGHEM - HAZEBROUCK Rd	23rd Aug		Work on road. Draughtmen Run. Training Orders Received. To take over from 2/0 & 7/3 Coys. 31st Division in the LA MOTTE SECTOR - S.O.S. on leave - Officers were named	8867.
GRASS CAMP (26/DQC6.3)	22nd Aug		Work in hand with officers of 2/0 D.C. Move to new Camp near HAZEBROUCK - divided amongst 11.30 am - 1 O.R. from Reinf.	8867
"	24 Aug		Work on Divisional Baths TIR ANGLAIS and other jobs. Company in Reserve working for Back area dumps. Effective strength 7 officers 209 ORs	8868
"	25th "		Work as above.	8868
"	26th "		do — 1 O.R. Reinforced from France	8867
"	27th "		do — 1 O.R. Leave to U.K. 1 O.R. from leave — 1 O.R. Pte LEWIS GUN COURSE LE TOUQUET	8868
"	28th "		do — 1 O.R. leave to U.K. 2 Officers and 51 ORs reported for work as part attached Works Company from 120 Fde. - Ranks, billets and rations with Field Company.	8868
"	29th "		Work as above - 100 R. b'tack up above party 6 C 2.0 mains and 61 ORs	8868
"	30th "		Work as above. — 1 Officer and 31 ORs Joined Company making up strength of Works Company to 3 Officers and 252 Rs.	8868
"	31st "		2 Section and Coy. HQars. returned to new VIEUX BERQUIN work in roads under O.C. 229 F.D. Company. Effective strength 7 Officers & all ORs attached 2 Offrs. and 72 ORs	8868

[signature] Major RE
O.C. 2/1st W.R. Co. RE
31/8/18

CONFIDENTIAL

WAR DIARY

231ST FIELD COMPANY. R.E.

September 1918

WAR DIARY
or
INTELLIGENCE SUMMARY

Army Form C. 2118

Place	Date	Hour	Summary of Events and Information	Remarks and references to Appendices
CAMP 34/DIGbz.9	1st September		Camp moves - Company in Reserve employed in preparing 40th Divisional Headquarters at LA MOTTE - Divisional Baths and General Salvage work - Demolition School taken over from O.C. 229th Field Company - 3 O.Rs proceeded to hospital	
" "	2nd "		Work as above - 1 O.R. returned from leave - 3 Sedan delates allowed to work as above	
" "	3rd "		do - 1 O.R. from R.E. School of Instruction ROUEN	
" "	4th "		do do - 1. O.R. to R.E. School of Instruction ROUEN - Lt POSTLETHWAITE proceeded	
" "	5th "		do do 1. O.R. to R.E. School of Instruction ROUEN	
" "	6th "		to XI Corps Officers' School HARDELOT (Rest Camp.) General Salvage work + Improvements to Camp - 1 O.R. returned from leave	
" "	7th "		Effective Strength of Company 7 Officers 307 O.Rs with 3 officers - 07 O.Rs 1st Field Works Camp employed attached.	
" "	8th "		Work as above. MAJOR VILLA proceeded on Special leave to U.K. - Commenced y	
" "	9th "		Work as above. Handed to Capt E.J. DOWSON R.E. from 9.0 am	
" "	10th "		Work as above. Company two 2 sections moved to L. s.r.a. 62 Road making and maintenance	
" "	11th "		" "	
" "	12th "		" 2. O.R. returned from leave to U.K. →	
" "	13th "		"	
" "	14th "		"	
" "	15th "		Effective strength 6 officers, 307 O.R. attachd 3 Officers, 1 O.R. proceeded on leave to U.K. 844 O.R H.Q. 2 sections + draught proceed march 27 E.z.z. 1 O.R returned from leave L POSTLETHWAITE returned from XII Corps Officers' School.	

WAR DIARY
or
INTELLIGENCE SUMMARY
(Erase heading not required.)

Army Form C. 2118

Instructions regarding War Diaries and Intelligence Summaries are contained in F.S. Regs., Part II and the Staff Manual respectively. Title Pages will be prepared in manuscript.

Place	Date	Hour	Summary of Events and Information	Remarks and references to Appendices
Camp Sept. A 27 c 22	Sept 16th		FIELD C.R.E. in Reserve. Road making & maintenance, Salvage, Construction of Baths & A.D.S. Temporary E.H. Bowman James Company for duty. 1 O.R. proceeded to Cadre School for Inf. Course.	EHB
"	17th		Work no alter. 1 O.R. proceeded as reinforcement from Base Depot. N.5. Section moved from D18 b 2 9 to Camp N 27 c 2 2	EHB
"	18th			EHB
"	19th		No. 4 Section moved from L5 a 6 2 to A 27 c 22	EHB
"	20th			EHB
"	21st			EHB
"	22nd			EHB
"	23rd			EHB
"	24th		Effects bought 7.0pm. Sold O.R. Stokes 3.0pm Sd. O.R.	EHB
"	25th		Work on Nieppe Sector taken over from 31st Division in accordance with O.O. No. 7. Order for Move (Later place in Move No. 2	EHB
"	26th		the morning of the 26th :- Major J. E. Villa MC, Ed returns from leave. (G B 18 a 4 2 Sheet 36 N.W. Edition 9A. Section moved G B7C 35½/15. Heavy enemy bombardment Headquarters & 4 Sections moved. 1 OR joined company from Base. the was slightly wounded. 1 O.R. wounded.	EHB
Camp B7C 35½/15 (Sheet 36 NW)	26th		Work on erecting Camouflage Screens in front of th. NIEPPE SYSTEM. RT 15 Bde. area	EHB
"	27th		do do with Effective Strength of Company of men. 208 O.R.'s attached 30.ft. 30 ors	EHB
"	28th		do do Erecting hedges across the RIVER WARNAVE and Roas Repairs forward	EHB
"	29th			EHB
"	30th		Work on erecting hedges across the RIVER WARNAVE and Road Repairs forward	EHB

Villa. Major R.E.
O.C. 731 Field Company.

30.9.'18.

CONFIDENTIAL.

WAR DIARY

231st (Field) Company, R.E.

October. 1918.

Vol - 29

WAR DIARY or INTELLIGENCE SUMMARY

Army Form C. 2118

Place	Date	Hour	Summary of Events and Information	Remarks and references to Appendices
Sheet 36.N.W B.7.C.55.15"	1st October		Work on Bridging and Repairs to Roads. – 10.R. returned from Leave. Transport lines moved to 36.N.W/A.16.b.5.4.	[sig]
"	2nd Oct.		Evacuation of LE BIZET and ARMENTIERES by the enemy. Coy. to a general reconnaissance for River LYS. Both Bridges by & aircraft made were forward – Orders received for River LYS. Both Bridges – all Bridges at Sheet 36 NW – C.15.d.6.8. to allow for the infantry crossing – all bridges having been reported as demolished. Transport arrangements made and completed on Bridge both taken trails at 4.0 am – arrived at bridge at LE BIZET 6.0 a.m. arrival at C.9.c.8.3. from which point the bridge had to be carried at hand with 2/3rd Bat. – Bridge complete 8.0. am 3rd Oct. at which time the Bnd. Dismantling Pcty. of the 119th Bde 40th Division crossed over the LYS.	[sig]
"	3rd.		Another crossing at C.19.C.7.8. between G.36.NW/B.12.B.4.4. work on roads Headquarters & 4 Sections moved in/1 R.A.M.C. attached for Water testing in forward trenches so as far as River LYS. -	[sig]
Sheet 36NW.3.W B.12.B.4.4	4		Work on roads pushed on as far as River LYS. – Filling Craters in B.9.C.5.5. – 1.02. 6 x 5" Coys. LE BIZET – Transport Divn moved to B.9.C.5.5. – 1.02. 6 x 5" Coys. LEWIS GUN SCHOOL at QUESQUES. – 119th Bde rushes for and obtained permission for a Pontoon Bridge for their across the River LYS at 36 NW/C.10d.9.1.	[sig]
"	5		Work completed by 1.10 pm at which time the bridge was ready to take Field artillery & machine guns. 1 Platoon attached Infantry moved to Sheet 36 NW (C.27.a1.8) One section A.M.S. I below to be attached to work in that area to be to Poilu Pontoon bridges. V. to be ready for repairing the bridges. They were	[sig]

WAR DIARY or INTELLIGENCE SUMMARY

Army Form C. 2118

Place	Date	Hour	Summary of Events and Information	Remarks and references to Appendices
Sheet 36 NW BriBu4	5th October		also instructed to defend the Bridge Head in the event of an enemy attack. Remainder of Company on Bridging & repairs to roads. Effective Strength of Company 7 officers - 208 O.Rs plus 3 officers 70 ORs attached works Company.	J.C.J.
H11 a.5.3	6th Oct.		LT. KNIGHT RE proceeded to XV Corps Gas School. - LT. BURT RE & RG School of Instruction ROUEN. - No 2 Section moved to join No 3 Section at C.27.a.1.8. while the remaining 2 sections, 2 platoons attached Infantry & Headquarters moved to H11 a.5.3 so as to be available for work on forward roads and to give assistance to the Defence Schemes of the Bdes in the line which was the 120th Bde.	J.C.J.
	7th Oct		LT. WILBURN rejoined Company from GRE's office where he was acting as assistant adjutant. — work on forward Roads from ROUEN.	J.C.J. J.C.O.
	8th "		Work on forward Roads. — 1 O.R. rejoined company RE annex ROUEN.	J.C.J.
	9th "		Work on forward Roads and Clearing Roads in ARMENTIERES. - LT. McTAVISH A. 11th Cameron Highlanders attached 23./.P.C. was wounded by shell fire - 2nd Lt. WILSON sent up to replace him. - 1 O.R. wounded and returned to duty.	
	10th "		No 2 Section withdrawn from C.27.a.1.8. & rejoined Company at H.11.a.5.3. Coy. is & section plus 1 platoon attached troops at C.27.a.7.8.	J.C.J.

1875. Wt. W593/826 1,000,000 4/15 J.B.C. & A. A.D.S.S./Forms/C. 2118.

WAR DIARY or INTELLIGENCE SUMMARY

Army Form C. 2118

Place	Date	Hour	Summary of Events and Information	Remarks and references to Appendices
H11a5.3	10th October (contd)		2 O.Rs. proceeded to 2nd Army Rest Camp - 1 O.R. proceeded on leave.	/607
"	11th	"	Work on Forward Roads and in ARMENTIERES - 4 O.Rs. returned from Rest Camp.	/607
"	12th	"	1 O.R. proceeded on leave. No.1 Section and K.O.S.B.'s relieved No.3 Section and K.O.Y.L.I.'s at NOUVELLE HOUPLINES. Capt. I.R. G.O.C. 46th Division inspected the 170th Works Company attached to this Company for work. - Effective Strength of Company Officers 7 - O.R.s 208	/607
"	13th	"	attached 30 Officers 769 O.R.s - 1 O.R. proceeded on leave. Work on Posts in Ouvrage Outpost Line - Work on Forward Roads. - 1 O.R. G. No. 9 R.E. Workshop Company for duty (authority - D.A.Q.M.G. N.57100/611 CE.E.7.10.15)	/607
"	14th	"	Work as above - Transport Lorry moved to Shed 36 NW H 4 of 4.3. Lt. KNIGHT returned from XV Corps Gas School. No. 2 Section - KOYLI's and Cameron Highlanders (attached) proceeded to forward billets at NOUVELLE HOUPLINES - Distribution of Company 2 Sections 3 platoon	/607
H11a5.3	15th	"	att. inf? at NOUVELLES HOUPLINES - 2 Sections and HQ at H11a5.3 HQ + 2 platoon moved to NOUVELLES HOUPLINES - Enemy enthroned on Ouvrage. Front commenced work on filling craters at Shed 36 NW C.80. Central Command	/607
NOUVELLE HOUPLINES sh36NWC27a18	16th	"	reads for transport the same evening. - Capt. DOWSON proceeded on leave to BOULOGNE.	789
sh36NWHb77	17th		Headquarters & selections and attached infantry moved to J.I.677 Sheet 36 NE. Transport Lorries moved to Sheet 36 NW C27a/.0	/607

1875 Wt. W593/826 1,000,000 4/15 J.B.C. &A. A.D.S.S./Forms/C. 2118.

Place	Date	Hour	Summary of Events and Information	Remarks and references to Appendices
SH.36NE/J6b7 Company	17th October		36NW / 2 Culverts demolished by enemy at C30 d 9.1 - repaired and roads for horsefoot Brucerine or Cralis + roads ready for horsefoot by 9.0 pm by 10.0 a.m.	X607
36NE/D30a77	18th Oct		That night as far as 36NE/D30 a 2.9. Headquarters & Sections and attached Infantry moved to 36NE/D30a77. 1 o.r. junior Company from Base Depot on Reinforcement. Bridging commenced across Canal at 36NE/D24c77 post. Took supplies by him - arrival of Bridging equipment. 2 Sections employed on Bridging & 2 Sections on repairing roads on N. Bank.	607 / 607
36NE/F27b99	19th Oct		O'Cond. & Section moved to 36NE/F27b99.9. For purposes of Bridging Canal DE ROUBAIX - Bruerin for Horse Transport only across Canal. Complete by 4.0 pm - Light Traffic Bridge commenced at 26NE/F21b05 Shanghami Amphib. bridge. 2 Sections at D30a77 employed on one to carry Horse Transport Co. Bridge of the point changed from on Shanghami Bridge commenced 1 o.r. proceeded on Leave. Effect strength 7 off. 205 o.rs. attached 3 off. 66 o.rs. one for carrying parties - work on Shanghami Bridge - work recommenced Bridge at F27b99 charges & Lorry Bridge - work recommenced Shanghami of Bridge at D30a77 in progress - bridge ready	607 / 607
F27b99	20th Oct		for use.	607

WAR DIARY
or
INTELLIGENCE SUMMARY
(Erase heading not required.)

Army Form C. 2118

Place	Date	Hour	Summary of Events and Information	Remarks and references to Appendices
ROUBAIX AREA F27 b.9.9. (Sheet 36)	21st October 1918		Work on finishing of LORRY BRIDGES at F27.b.9.9 and D.30.a.7.7 — Repairing Roads from D.30.a.7.7 to WAMBECHIES. — 2 Sections still at D.20.a.7.7.	App. 87.
"	22nd		Nos 2 & 4 Section & Transport lines formed Company at F27.b.9.9 (Sheet 36) — Bridge at F27.b.9.9 opened for traffic for 8½ ton (heavy loads) from XV Corps School.	App. 87.
"	23rd		Work as above — I.O.R. proceeded on leave 15% U.K. 2 O.Rs returned from U.K. Driver	App. 87.
"	24th		Work as above — Warning order received 3rd Division in relief 26/27	App. 87.
"	25th		Work as above. Company Orders received to Division relieving 3rd Division on night 26 & U.K. — No 4 Section moved Capt LINDERMERE relieved Capt WATNEY proceeding on leave & U.K. — This company is not relieving another	App. 87.
			as advanced party 6 H.Q. central Sheet 37.	App. 87.
LEERS NORD AREA H.8 Central (Sheet 37)	26th		Field Company relieved by 3rd Division. Advanced Infantry moved to H.8. central — Effective Headquarters 3 Sections & advanced Infantry 3 Officers 65 O.Rs.	App. 87.
"	27th		Strength of the Company 7 Officers 204 O.Rs, attached Infantry 3 Officers & NCOs & NCOs went Company Rest Day. Church Service 10.30 am.	App. 87.
"	28/29th		Hers area. Attempts made to cross CANAL D'ESCAULT at 37/C.20 d.17. and 37/C.20 d.79 failure owing to the enemy machine gun and Artillery fire. Any attempt at Bridging brought down artillery and machine gun fire. — I O.R. wounded by shell-fire at B.20.d.7.9 — 10R proceeded on leave U.K.	App. 87. App. 87.
"	30th		CANAL D'ESCAULT Bridged by a Tin Roof Bridge at C.20 c.8.5 at 3.30 am — Slight enemy fire on leave on Canal Bank at C.20.d.1.7.	App. 87.
"	31st		31st October at about B20d.7.9. Another Footbridge was thrown across the ESCAULT between midnight and 3 am.	App. 87.

31.10.18

[signature]
O.C. 131st Fd Company

—Confidential—

War Diary

231st (Field) Company, R.E.

November, 1918.

WAR DIARY
or
INTELLIGENCE SUMMARY
(Erase heading not required.)

Army Form C. 2118

Place	Date	Hour	Summary of Events and Information	Remarks and references to Appendices
LEERS NORD (H6 central) SHEET 37	1st November		4 Sections employed on Roads, preparation of Bridges at Brunip and manoeuvres of Footbridges across the SCHELDT RIVER — No 2 Section moved to Advance Billets at WARCOING.	
"	2nd	"	Work as above Effective Strength — 7 Officers — 202 ORs attached 10 Officers — 65 ORs	
"	3rd	"	Work as above.	
"	4th	"	"	
"	5th	"	Work as above. Trestle taken up to WARCOING for HEAVY TRESTLE Bridging across the River Scheldt— Lt Burt CG approved plans— Re School ROUEN. — 2/Lt J.C. GRASSIE joined Company from	
"	6th	"	River Scheldt— preparation for Heaving Footbridge across the canal in view of operations which are to commence on the 10th Nov 1918 — No 4 Section relieved No 2 Section at WARCOING	
"	7th	"	Our Footbridge thrown across the River Scheldt— within our approach— Lt KENNEDY joined Company from Britain	
"	8th	"	Enemy withdrew on dual front. Pack ANIMAL Bridge thrown across the River WARCOING	
WARCOING	9th	"	SCHELDT Completed by 5.0 p.m. 9.11.16 — HQ and 4 Section now located WARCOING Effective Strength 9 Offs—201 ORs attached 1 Offs—67 ORs	
"	10th	"	Transport lines removed at H3 central. Heavy Pony Bridge across the River Scheldt started at 37/C20d.3.7.	
"	11th	"	Work on Heavy Pony Bridge and approach Roads took continues— News of the Armistice being Signed officially reached the Company at 11.5 am — Work on heavy bridge carried on until — 4 O.P.s reinforcement from Base Depot	
"	12th	"	Work on Heavy Pony Bridge continues	
"	13th	"	do do Transport lines joins the Company at WARCOING	

WAR DIARY
or
INTELLIGENCE SUMMARY
(Erase heading not required.)

Army Form C. 2118

Place	Date	Hour	Summary of Events and Information	Remarks and references to Appendices
LA MADELINE (34/K21c83) " (36/K29a95)	26th Nov.		A Section employed on reconstructing LILLE-ROUBAIX Main Line. 1 O.R. proceeded on leave	(30)
"	27th	"	Company moved to a more suitable billet at K29a95. 1 O.R. proceeded on leave to U.K.	(30)
"	28th	"	Work as above. 1 O.R. proceeded on leave to U.K. 1 O.R. returning from leave.	(30)
"	29th	"	Company employed on dismantling demolished bridge at 36/K23 central under C.R.E. XV Corps Troops. 1 O.R. proceeded on leave. 2 O.R.s proceeded to attend a Stabilising Bituminous Workshop WAMBRECHIES	(30)
"	30th	"	In Continuity & Journey Work as above. Effective Strength 8 Officers and 301 O.R.s	(30)

[signature] Major R.E.
O.C. 231st O.C.
30/11/18

CONFIDENTIAL

WAR DIARY.

231st (Field) Coy. R.E.

December 1918.

Army Form C. 2118

WAR DIARY
or
INTELLIGENCE SUMMARY
(Erase heading not required.)

Instructions regarding War Diaries and Intelligence Summaries are contained in F. S. Regs., Part II. and the Staff Manual respectively. Title Pages will be prepared in manuscript.

Place	Date	Hour	Summary of Events and Information	Remarks and references to Appendices
ST MAURICE (LILLE - 36/K29q95)	1st December		Company Employed under C.R.E. XVth Corps Troops in renewal of Clumbelus Bridge at cross main thoroughfare. - Lt GRASSIE proceeds to 2110th A. Dn: Workshops	867
"	2nd	"	WAMBRECHIES. - Company Rest day.	867
"	"	"	Work as above. 2 O.Rs leave to U.K. - 1 O.R. to Hospital	867
"	3rd	"	do do 2 O.Rs leave to U.K.	867
"	4th	"	do do 4 O.R. leave to U.K. - 1 O.R. returns from leave	867
"	5th	"	do do 1 O.R. leave to U.K. - 1 O.R. " "	867
"	6th	"	do do 1 O.R. " " - 1 O.R. to Hospital	867
"	7th	"	do do 2 O.Rs from leave. Effective Strength – Visit of King GEORGE V to this area. Company gave a holiday. Saw the roads at 3.30 pm (Boulainville) Centenary of Waterloo.	867
"	8th	"	Company Rest Day. - 40th Div: Inspection of men proceeding on leave. Reservists attended 11. a.m.	86
"	"	"	This company detailed a representative Party. Y/CH: BEIGHTON Awarded CROIX DE GUERRE with Star. - Lt BURT O.C. returns from leave	86
"	9th	"	Work under CRE XVth Corps Troops - Removal of Demolished Bridge - 1 OR to U.K.	86
"	10th	"	Work as above - 1 O.R. on leave to U.K. Repair Sharp, ROUEN - S.O.Rs (Minera)	867
"	11th	"	Work as above -- 3 O.Rs to Steam. Repair Shop - 2 O.Rs from leave	867
"	12th	"	demolished - 2 O.Rs on leave to U.K. - 2 O.Rs from leave.	867
"	13th	"	Work as above - 1 O.R. (Miner Demolitions) - 1 O.R. to U.K. - 2 O.Rs	865
"	"	"	Work as above Capt J.G. Voce proceeds on leave to U.K. - 1 O.R. on leave - 2 O.Rs (Miners) demobilised	

WAR DIARY or INTELLIGENCE SUMMARY

Army Form C. 2118

Place	Date	Hour	Summary of Events and Information	Remarks and references to Appendices
St MAURICE (LILLE 36/K29 a 9.3)	14th Dec?		Work under CRE XV Corps Troops - Neuvelles Bridge, Reserval Shelter Shingles 7 Officers - 193 ORs - attached 11 ORs	
"	15th		2 ORs on leave to UK - 2 ORs to CRE for Demob Duties - 1 OR G.S.O.P. - 1 OR from leave Company Rest Day - Representative Party sent to Special Church Service at ROUBAIX - 1 OR on leave to UK	
"	16th		Work under CRE XV Corps Troops - 1 OR on leave to UK	
"	17th		Work as above - 2 ORs on leave to UK - 1 OR from leave - 1 OR G.Troop - 6 (nine) demobilised	
"	18th		Work as above - 1 OR on leave to UK - 1 OR Gen Personnel Employment	
"	19th		Company for temporary duties as loader - 1 OR from leave. Work as above - 1 OR on leave to UK - 1 OR from leave	
"	20th		Work as above - 1 OR on leave to UK - 2 ORs from leave	
"	21st		Work as above - 1 OR from Hosp. Shelter Shingle 7 Captain 7 Officers 186 ORs attached 11 ORs	
"	22nd		Company Rest Day - 2 ORs to leave to UK - 2 ORs from leave	
"	23rd		Work under CRE XV Corps Troops - 2 ORs to leave to UK - 1 OR from leave	
"	24th		Hook keeper Company Rest Day - 2 ORs to leave to UK - Lt KNIGHT on leave to UK	
"	25th		Nowrk. Christmas Day - 3 ORs on leave to UK - 15.	
"	26th		No work. Boxing Day - 4 ORs invalided to leave to UK	

WAR DIARY
or
INTELLIGENCE SUMMARY

(Erase heading not required.)

Army Form C. 2118

Place	Date	Hour	Summary of Events and Information	Remarks and references to Appendices
30/K 29.9.5	27 Dec.		Work under CRE & "G" Corps Troops Completed. Company was working under CRE 40th Division — 1 O.R. proceeded on leave to U.K.	(Es)
"	28 "		Work on demolitions of roads & stone huts etc — 1 O.R. demobilised — 2 O.Rs. from leave. Effective strength 7 officers — 185 O.Rs.	(Es)
"	29 "		Company Rest Day — 2 O.Rs. leave to U.K. — 5 O.Rs. from leave — Capt. Voce returned from leave to U.K.	(Es)
"	30 "		Work in Camp — 1 O.R. to hospital — 4 O.Rs. reinforcement from Base.	(Es)
"	31 "		do. 3 O.Rs. leave to U.K. — 1 O.R. demobilised	(Es)

3/1/19

[signature]
Major R.E.
O.C. 231st Field Co.

WR 32

469

CONFIDENTIAL.

WAR DIARY

231ST (FIELD) Co. R.E

January 1919.

WAR DIARY or INTELLIGENCE SUMMARY

Army Form C. 2118.

(Erase heading not required.)

Place	Date	Hour	Summary of Events and Information	Remarks and references to Appendices
St MAURICE 36/K290.95	1st JANUARY 1919		Work in Camp - 3 ORs demobilised - 4 ORs joined Company from Base as Reinforcements, 3 ORs on leave to UK	SEO
"	2nd "	"	do do do 2 ORs demobilised - 20 ORs on leave to UK	SEO
"	3rd "	"	do do do 3 ORs on leave	SEO
"	4th "	"	do do do 1 OR on leave. Effective Strength of Company 7 officers 185 ORs	SEO
"	5th "	"	Company Rest Day - Arms inspected - Church Parade - 3 ORs returned from leave - 2 ORs on leave	SEO
"	6th "	"	Work in Camp - 3 ORs from leave - 2 ORs demobilised - Lt KENNEDY proceeded on Kings leave to UK - 1 OR demobilised	SEO
"	7th "	"	Work in Camp - 1 OR on leave to UK - Sergt BUCKBY proceeded on Kings leave to UK - 1 OR demobilised	SEO
"	8th "	"	4 ORs Reinforcements from Base.	SEO
"	9th "	"	Work in Camp - 4 ORs from leave - 2 ORs on leave - 1 OR demobilised	SEO
"	10th "	"	do 5 ORs demobilised - 2 ORs on leave	SEO
"	11th "	"	do 2 ORs on leave to UK - 1 OR demobilised	SEO
"	12th "	"	Company Rest Day. 3 ORs demobilised Effective Strength 9 Company 7 Officers 183 ORs	SEO
"	13th "	"	Work in Camp - 2 ORs from leave - 1 OR on leave to UK - Church Parade	SEO
"	14th "	"	do 3 ORs demobilised - 1 OR from leave	SEO
"	15th "	"	do 1 OR on leave to UK	SEO
"	16th "	"	do 1 OR on leave to UK	SEO
"	17th "	"	do 2 ORs on leave to UK	SEO
"	18th "	"	do 1 OR on leave to UK	SEO
"	19th "	"	do 1 OR demobilised - 1 OR on leave Effective Strength 7 Officers 177 ORs	SEO
"	19th "	"	Company Rest Day - 8 ORs demobilised - Church Parade - Ryles unpacked	SEO
"	20th "	"	Work on Class "B" Bridge at 26/F23c65". 1 OR from leave - 1 OR on leave to UK	SEO
"	"	"	15 ORs demobilised	SEO
"	21st "	"	Work on Bridge at 26/F23c65". 1 OR leave to UK - 5 OR demobilised	SEO
"	22nd "	"	Work on Bridge - 2 ORs on leave - 2 ORs returned from leave at base - 2 ORs leave	SEO
"	22nd "	"	3 ORs demobilised	SEO
"	23rd "	"	Work on Bridge - 10 ORs demobilised	SEO
"	24th "	"	Work on Bridge - 1 OR on leave to UK - Lt KENNEDY returned from leave	SEO
"	25th "	"	Work on Bridge. 2 ORs demobilised - 2 ORs 10 joined Company	SEO
"	"	"	from Base Effective Strength 9 Company 7 Officers - 162 ORs	SEO

Army Form C. 2118.

WAR DIARY
or
INTELLIGENCE SUMMARY.
(Erase heading not required.)

Instructions regarding War Diaries and Intelligence Summaries are contained in F.S. Regs., Part II. and the Staff Manual respectively. Title pages will be prepared in manuscript.

Place	Date	Hour	Summary of Events and Information	Remarks and references to Appendices
ST MAURICE 36/K=9 a.9.5	26th January 1919		Company Rest Day - Rifle Inspection -	
"	27th Jany		Work on Bridge - 2 ORs on leave to UK - 20 ORs joined Company for Reinforcements	
"	28th "		Work on Bridge - 1 OR on leave to UK - LT GRASSIE to Hospital	
"	29th "		Work on Bridge - 1 OR from leave - 2 ORs sick - 6 ORs demobilised	
"	30th "		Work on Bridge - 10 ORs leave to UK.	
"	31st "		Work on Bridge - 10 ORs leave to UK	

Stolle.
Major. R.E.
O.C. 231st Aus Coy R.E.

1/2/19

WB 231

465M

CONFIDENTIAL

WAR DIARY

231ˢᵗ FIELD COMPANY·R·E·

FEBRUARY·1919

VOL. 29

Army Form C. 2118.

WAR DIARY
or
INTELLIGENCE SUMMARY.
(Erase heading not required.)

Instructions regarding War Diaries and Intelligence Summaries are contained in F. S. Regs., Part II. and the Staff Manual respectively. Title pages will be prepared in manuscript.

Place	Date	Hour	Summary of Events and Information	Remarks and references to Appendices
ST. MAURICE 36/K20 a 9-5.	1st February		Work on "B" Class Steel Girder Bridge at F.23.c.6.5. — 1.OR leaves O.R. Effect. Strength s/Or 7 Off. 129 ors	See
"	2nd	"	Work as above — Company Rest day — Inspection of Rifles — Kits etc. — 1. OR Leave to U.K.	See
"	3rd	"	Work as above — 1. OR Leave to U.K.	See
"	4th	"	Work as above — Lt. BONHAM K.E. and 1 O.R. proceeded on Leave to U.K.	See
"	5th	"	Work as above — 1. OR Leave to U.K.	See
"	6th	"	Work as above — 1. OR Leave to U.K.	See
"	7th	"	Work as above — 1. OR Leave to U.K. — 2 ORs returned from Leave — 1. OR demobilised	See
"	8th	"	Work as above — 1. OR Leave to U.K. — 2 ORs returned from Leave Effective Strength of Coy. 7 off — 128 ors Leave U.K. — 6 ORs demobilised	See
"	9th	"	Work as above — Company Rest Day — Inspection of Rifles Kits etc. — 2 ORs Leave U.K. — 6 ORs demobilised	See
"	10th	"	Work as above — 1 O.R. Leave to U.K. — 5 ORs returned from Leave — 2 ORs demobilised.	See
"	11th	"	Work as above — 2 ORs from Leave	See
"	12th	"	Work as above — 1. OR Leave to U.K. — 3 ORs from Leave	See
"	13th	"	Work as above — 1 OR on Leave to U.K. — 1 OR from Leave	See
"	14th	"	Work as above	See
"	15th	"	Work as above — Capt. VOCE transferred to 239" Fd. Company — 2 ORs demobilised — 2 ORs from Leave Effective Strength — 6 Officers — 117 ORs. Orders received (Exhort from XV Corps No.667/20(G) of 12.2.19) of Transfer of 231" Field Company from 40" Division to 3rd Division on Relief of 58" Field Coy". 36" Div. on Gunner. To await details from above.	See

WAR DIARY
or
INTELLIGENCE SUMMARY.
(Erase heading not required.)

Army Form C. 2118.

Place	Date	Hour	Summary of Events and Information	Remarks and references to Appendices
ST AMAURICE 36/K20.a.9.5	16" Feb		No work. Company Rest Day. Inspection of Rifles, Kits etc - 2 O.Rs demobilised	Feb
"	17"	"	Work on Bridges at 36/F23.c.6.5 - Bridge launched to temporary arrangements made for Launching over boxes	Feb
"			Launching over work 6.229. L/Z Koomboy & L/GRAHAM & 220. F.C. transport 2 Or hwalnwer 1 OR Fairfax	Feb
"	18"	"	Work on Bridges completed so far as we are concerned - Launching completed successfully. 1 OR leave 3 day from Leave	Feb
"	19"	"	Work on Bridge handed over to 229 Field Company. Re. Company Supplys in clearing equipment	Feb
"			etc. - 2 ORs returned from leave.	
"	20"	"	Company Employed in clearing equipment etc. - L/BOWMAN returned from leave - 2 ORs from leave	Feb
"	21"	"	Work as above - 2 ORs from leave	Feb
"	22nd	"	Work as above - 1 OR leave to U.K. - 6 ORs transferred to 229" Field Company Eff. Strength 3 Off. 112 ORs	Feb
"	23rd	"	"Work as above - Company Rest Day - Inspection of Rifles Kits etc-	Feb
"	24"	"	Work as above - 2 ORs from leave	Feb
"	25"	"	Work as above - 1 OR from leave	Feb
"	26"	"	Work as above 1 OR leave to U.K.	Feb
"	27"	"	Work as above -	Feb
"	28"	"	Work as above -	Feb

J.Griffin Major R.E.
O.C. 231st Field Company
28.2.19.

Army Form C. 2118.

WAR DIARY
or
INTELLIGENCE SUMMARY

(Erase heading not required.)

Instructions regarding War Diaries and Intelligence Summaries are contained in F. S. Regs., Part II. and the Staff Manual respectively. Title pages will be prepared in manuscript.

Place	Date	Hour	Summary of Events and Information	Remarks and references to Appendices
ST MAURICE FRANCE 36/K 20.a.9.5	1st March	-	Company employed on cleaning equipment etc. Effective Strength of Coy. 3 Off. 105 OR.	B3
"	2nd	-	No Work weekend Coy. rest day. Inspection of Rifles and Kits.	B3
"	3rd	-	Company employed on cleaning equipment and checking stores	B3
	4th	-	Work as above. 1 OR Leave to U.K.	B3
	5th	-	Work as above. 1 OR Leave to U.K. 5# ORs transferred from 224th Field Coy RE. 4 ORs transferred from 224th Field Coy RS. 31 ORs transferred to 224 Fld Coy RE. 32 ORs transferred to 229 Fld Coy RE	B3
	6th	-	Work as above. 1 OR Leave to U.K.	B3
	7th	-	Work as above 1 OR Leave to U.K	B3
	8th	-	Work as above. 1 OR returned back from leave to U.K. Effective Strength 3 Off. 22 OR.	B3
	9th	-	No Work. Coy. rest day. Inspection of Rifles	B3
	10th	-	Company employed on work in Camp and checking equipment	B3
	11th	-	Work as above 1 OR returned from leave to U.K	B3
	12th	-	Work as above 2/Lt T.C. Nottingham transferred from 224th H.Bat Coy R.E. and reported for duty "2/Lt R.L. Brown " " - 233 K Fld. Coy RE " " - "	B3
	13th	-	Work as above. 10R transferred from 229th Fld Coy	B3
	14th	-	Work as above	B3
	15th	-	Work as above. 1 OR from leave U.K. Effective Strength 5 Off. 23 OR.	B3
	16th	-	No Work. Coy. Rest day. Inspection of Rifles. 1 OR from leave to U.K	B3

WAR DIARY
or
INTELLIGENCE SUMMARY.
(Erase heading not required.)

Army Form C. 2118.

Place	Date	Hour	Summary of Events and Information	Remarks and references to Appendices
ST. MAURICE FRANCE 36/K 20.A.9.5.	17th March		Work in Camp.	
	18th		Work as above. 1 O.R. proceed transferred from 224th Fld Coy R.E on Sick leave in U.K.	
	19th		Work as above. 1 Lt R.W. Fitch transferred from 129 Fld Coy R.E. and reported for duty. 30 O.Rs transferred from 34th Division R.E.'s	
	20th		Work as above. 102 back from leave. 62 O.Rs transferred from 14th Division R.E.	
	21st		Work as above	
	22nd		Rifle and Kit Inspection. Effective Strength 7 O/rs. 115 O.Rs.	
	23rd		No Work. Coy Rest Day. Rifle Inspection. 1 O.R. returned from leave to U.K.	
	24th		Drill, physical training and games.	
	25th		As above. 1 O.R. struck off strength after 7 days in hospital. 1 O.R. from leave to U.K.	
	26th		As above. Major Villar on leave to U.K. 1 O.R. transferred from 150th Field Coy R.E.	
	27th		No work. 1 Lt J. Gross struck off strength. Sent to hospital on leave in U.K. 1 O.R. from leave to U.K.	
	28th		As above. 2 O.Rs to Hospital. Orders received to proceed to relieve 35th Infty R.S	
	29th		Nation Division Germany on 29.3.19. Entrained at Prevo ville 16.00 hours reported 18.00 hours Effective Strength 6 off. 115 O.Rs	
	30th		Travelling	
	31st		Arrived at Nappe (Cologne) 4.00 hours. Detrained 12.00 hours reported to C.R.E. Nation Division for duty.	

231 7a C C9.
Mar 1919

www.ingramcontent.com/pod-product-compliance
Lightning Source LLC
Chambersburg PA
CBHW081545160426

43191CB00011B/1843